PONY TREKKING

PONY TREKKING

GLENDA SPOONER

B.E.F. Medal of Honour
B.H.S. Diploma

With drawings by
JOAN WANKLYN

J. A. ALLEN
LONDON

ISBN ◊ 85131 246 2

This revised edition published 1976 by
J. A. Allen & Company Limited,
1 Lower Grosvenor Place,
Buckingham Palace Road,
London, SW1W 0EL.

First published by Museum Press.

PRINTED IN GREAT BRITAIN BY
R. J. ACFORD LTD., INDUSTRIAL ESTATE,
CHICHESTER, SUSSEX

Contents

Illustrations

Half-Tone Illustrations

CHAPTER I

Trekking and Riding Holidays

NEW movements are nearly always exploited by the "hope-to-get-rich-quick" folk, and trekking and riding holidays are no exception.

Many centres which cater for these holidays are excellently run by well-qualified persons, experienced in horsemanship, able to instruct and knowing the right equipment to use, but owing to the overwhelming demand for this type of recreation in which the general public can participate Trekking and Riding Holiday Centres have sprung up like mushrooms all over the countryside. Very many of them are run by completely inexperienced persons using unsuitable animals and equipment, with the result that this excellent recreation is being exploited. Members of the public who attend these so-called riding centres complain of the conditions in them. Trekkers return from their holidays disillusioned, feeling that all is not well with the horses and ponies given them to ride, but, because of their lack of knowledge, they are unable to do anything about it. Should they venture to point out obvious lamenesses or sore backs under the saddle, they are given to understand that they know nothing about it and that everything is quite in order. Others complain of hard, uncomfortable saddles, broken straps, and of horses and ponies without shoes. Adults complain of being given under-sized or too-young ponies to ride which are suitable only for children, presumably because they are cheaper to buy and must earn their keep.

It was therefore suggested by the periodicals which received these complaints that some sort of supervision and inspection was needed, and that the Ponies of "Britain", with its international reputation and expert knowledge of ponies, was the ideal organization to undertake this service to the public and to the horses and ponies involved. Accordingly, early in 1959, the Committee of the Club appointed a panel of judges specially chosen for their sound practical knowledge. All Trekking and Riding Holiday Centres were then invited to afford these judges free access to their establishments so that Certificates of Approval could be awarded to those which achieved the desired standard. The response was extremely good. Most of the well-run, reputable centres immediately opened their doors and were both courteous and co-operative. As a result forty-five out of the fifty-four centres which our judges duly inspected in 1959 were awarded these certificates, which are greatly prized.

To be awarded a Certificate, establishments must attain 70% efficiency, preferably more. All Certificates are renewable annually. A list of centres which have received a Certificate of Approval from the Ponies of Britain is obtainable from Brookside Farm, Ascot, Berks., price 35p.

Objects of this Book

This book deals only with the treatment and care of the ponies/horses and their equipment and with the instruction which should be expected in trekking and riding holiday centres respectively throughout the country, and *not* with the accommodation of the riders themselves.

Its objects are:

1. To add to the pleasure of this wonderful recreation by supplying the added interest and colour which a little knowledge of this subject can bring.
2. To describe—
   (a) The types of horses and ponies best suited for this work.
   (b) the correct and most practical equipment to use and its care, so ensuring maximum comfort and safety of both horse/pony and rider.
   (c) the elementary instruction which is essential to the

enjoyment and comfort of the rider and his horse/pony.

3. To help people to recognize a well-run centre and to encourage a standard which ensures the well-being of the horses and ponies employed, with hope of eliminating the bad, sometimes deplorable, conditions prevailing in some quarters.

N.B. It is fully appreciated that there are several ways of doing the same thing. Trekking and riding holiday operators and instructors may not have the same methods; they may go about things differently, but provided the result is good, how it is achieved does not matter.

It is obviously impossible to include all these various methods in one book which, moreover, is designed not to teach people of experience and knowledge, but simply to act as a guide and encouragement to complete beginners and novices and to enable them to avoid the pitfalls, and so to start their holidays with a little knowledge and a few useful tips which it is hoped will add to their enjoyment.

Trekking

Trek is a Cape-Dutch word, from the Dutch, meaning "to move off" or go on a journey. Also commonly used by the Afrikaaners to denote time or distance, e.g. "four hours' trek from here", and in the old days it was measured by the speed of ox-wagons or Cape Carts.

"Trekking" in this country is, of course, quite different, but it gives the same feeling of adventure. It is a comparatively recent "recreation", which has a great deal to recommend it and has rapidly grown in popularity. It fulfils the desire of townspeople with no experience whatever of the country to see the countryside and to enjoy the wide open spaces. Even complete novices, whatever their age, sex or size—who have never even sat on a donkey on the sands— can go out trekking, and do so in safety and with confidence provided they patronize only reputable establishments. The benefit they derive from this exercise and healthy outdoor life is great.

They are also able to see our beautiful countryside at close quarters, and not just on picture postcards or from a car. Instead of laboriously climbing up on foot, they can ride up and down mountains with a minimum of effort. Panoramic views lie before them. They can visit the romantic but historical places of these islands where men like the great Marquis of Montrose, William Wallace, Robert Bruce, Rob Roy and Bonnie Prince Charlie earned their legendary fame. They can put back the clock to the days of the Druids, can ride along roads made centuries ago by the Roman Legions, see the famous Wall the Emperor Hadrian built across northern England, explore the old drove roads along which for generations the forbears of the ponies they ride carried the lead from mines to the seaports. The heather hills and the moors of Exmoor, the high Tors of Devon and the shady glades of the New Forest—long the hunting ground of kings—are theirs to enjoy. On the Black Mountain of Wales they can behold in their natural surroundings the famous Welsh Mountain ponies which, along with our other native breeds, are in such demand both at home and overseas, and fetch such high prices.

When on "trek" one should really ride a distance, camp out overnight and ride on the next day and so on for varying periods of time, 2–5 days, a week, or even longer. This is called "post-trekking" (see page 111) and should not be undertaken by beginners or the inexperienced whose muscles, being unused to this exercise, naturally get very stiff and sore. For this reason, and also because of the added expense and considerable organization required, "post-trekking" is undertaken by very few, if any, trekking centres.

Most operators in this country therefore only provide "day" treks, that is, they leave early in the morning, stopping at midday for a rest and sandwich lunch and, making a circular tour, return in the late afternoon or evening to headquarters. A different route is planned each day to give a variety of scenery. Trekking should be undertaken almost entirely at walking pace with short intervals of trotting where the ground is suitable and if those taking part are sufficiently experienced. Faster paces do not come under the heading of "trekking" but under "hacking" which in turn comes under Riding Holidays. The majority of people attending trekking centres are novices of all ages, sexes and sizes, but mostly young people. They greatly enjoy this recreation and the companionship of people and ponies without wishing for anything more than the most elementary instruction, and because of the nature of the country ridden over, it is more often than not impossible to proceed faster than a walk. But ponies are great walkers and surefooted as mountain goats. They are also very beautiful with their abundant manes and tails and varied colouring. All trekking should be leisurely as it was in a more romantic age—those who crave speed should ride motor-bikes!

Trekking is seasonal and centres operate with a few exceptions only in the summer months—from April to the end of October. Riding Holiday establishments operate all the year round.

What to Expect on "Trek"

Trekking parties should always expect to be accompanied by one or more instructors, one of whom acts as guide, generally the trekking operator himself, who usually owns the ponies, of which he is, or should be, justly proud. Some operators, especially in Wales, hire the ponies from farmers for the duration of the season, the week or per day as the case may be, which is not nearly so satisfactory from either the public's or the pony's point of view, as they do not take the same interest in hirelings as they do in their own animals.

Where the majority going out on trek or for a ride are novices, there should be an experienced and reliable instructor to every eight, ten or twelve riders. No trek or ride should go out unattended. It is also a great advantage if the person in charge also has a knowledge of the countryside as well as of ponies and horses, and is experienced in looking after novice riders and beginners.

As the trekking public are quite as much interested in seeing and exploring the countryside and in friends met and made, as in what and how they ride, instruction in trekking centres is only very elementary. Much more of course should be expected on riding holidays.

At the same time, novices are frequently so "smitten" that they later take up riding seriously as a direct result of having first tasted its joys and excitements on a trekking holiday. It is also noticeable that many complete novices who, when they arrive at a centre are, to put it in their own words, "scared stiff of horses and ponies", come to love them. They make friends with the pony that has carried them and return to that particular establishment because that pony is there. Many equine as well as human friends are made on trekking holidays.

Riding Holidays

Considerably more instruction in riding and in horse- and ponymastership should be expected and given at a Riding Holiday establishment. All properly organized riding holiday centres should most certainly have an enclosed space for use as a riding school, and those giving more advanced instruction, a covered school for use in all weathers. Instructors should be persons of long practical experience in the art of teaching riding so that the holiday-makers can derive maximum benefit and pleasure from this golden opportunity of a concentrated week or fortnight devoted to everything appertaining to the care, handling and riding of horses and ponies.

On riding holidays, those taking part should expect to be taken to see hunter trials, shows, meets of hounds and other horse activities, and sometimes even to participate in them. In other words they should expect to be encouraged in all aspects of horse- and ponymastership and to come away with an increased knowledge of the subject.

CHAPTER II

Centres and their Organization

TODAY completely unversed persons with no qualifications, even young girls straight from school, can start up in the riding business, sometimes without enough capital to feed their animals or to buy proper equipment, and with little or no knowledge to transmit. The risk that some parents run with their children is amazing and can only be attributed to ignorance. The instruction given, the condition of the animals used and the tatty, often dangerous (because liable to break) equipment, indicate how the public is being exploited by these "so-called" riding schools; and some trekking and riding centres are no exception. The organization dealt with below is the kind to be expected in well-run centres.

Advance Bookings

This is usually undertaken by either the operator or by the hotel or inn, or, in the case of Youth Movements, by the organization running them.

All centres should have a brochure setting out clearly their amenities, schedule, daily routine and what their charges are. These usually include the cost of the trekking and riding holidays but sometimes these are given separately. It is helpful if these brochures give some description of the countryside and the kind and size of animal supplied.

They should always state whether or not instruction is given, and in the case of riding holidays, what qualifications the instructors have, and what other activities are offered.

Form to Fill In

In trekking centres where large numbers are dealt with weekly or fortnightly (according to the booking), the name of the trekking operator should be given, the number of ponies kept and approximately how many go out on "trek" at a time and with how many instructors in attendance.

Many of the best centres send a form which they ask prospective clients to fill in, giving their name and address, height, weight in riding clothes, and previous equitation experience, if any. This is used as a guide to suitable mounts and instruction needed.

It is also important to discover before going whether or not guests are expected/encouraged/or not permitted to catch up the ponies, groom, saddle them, etc., or whether experienced staff are employed for this. Only thus can you know where to go and what clothes to take with you.

Where Trekking takes Place

In England, trekking mainly takes place in Devon and Somerset (i.e. Exmoor and Dartmoor), some in Cornwall; the New Forest in Hampshire, the Lake District, the fells and dales of Northumberland, Cumberland and Westmorland and the Hope Valley in Derbyshire. All over Wales, but particularly in the Black Mountain district of Brecon. In Scotland, the gorgeous Trossachs in Perthshire, the mountains and glens of Inverness-shire, Argyll and Aberdeen; the Border counties of Roxburghshire, Midlothian and also in Clackmannanshire, the Ochill and Eildon Hills and the Pennine Range.

All these various terrains have their characteristics and landmarks. All have their individual charm and interest, and there are approved trekking centres at each of them.

Riding holidays are not confined to any one district but are catered for in establishments all over England, Scotland and Wales, especially in England.

Well-run Establishments

Unless approved over a period of time, every centre is inspected by Ponies of Britain representatives annually. The Club takes no responsibility for the quality of board and lodging offered to riders but gives some idea of what accommodation is available and that the centre has a licence. If the required standard of the trekking/riding holidays offered is not over 70% a certificate is not awarded, and where held can be removed at any time. A new list is available in December of the preceding year.

Organizations of course differ, and these are the various arrangements which may be expected:

1. Hotels where the management run their own trekking centres, own their own ponies and equipment and employ a qualified and experienced instructor to be in charge.
2. Hotels which have an arrangement with an operator, who then runs their trekking or riding holiday centre for them, supplies the ponies, their equipment, food, shoes, etc., and himself takes charge, and/or has qualified and experienced staff, and pays them himself. He is therefore responsible for arranging the rides and for the safety of the riders.
3. Establishments—whether they cater for trekking or riding holidays or both—where the guests live in and are catered for either by the operator's wife and family, or by persons employed by them. Only those taking part in the riding are accommodated. The operator owns and runs the riding department.
4. Centres which accommodate the guests in hotel rooms or guest houses in nearby villages and provide the riding facilities only.
5. Establishments which leave the guests to make their own boarding arrangements and only provide riding or trekking facilities.
6. Youth Hostels—information can be obtained from the

Central Council of Physical Recreation, the Sports Council, 70 Brompton Road, London, SW3 3IX, the English Tourist Board, 4 Grosvenor Gardens, SW1 or travel agencies. A full descriptive list is available from Ponies of Britain, Brookside Farm, Ascot, Berks. SL5 7LU. Price 35p. A shorter list is also available, price 20p.

The best of these organizations place their trekking and riding holiday arrangements in the hands of an expert and either employ him to run their riding department for them, or recommend their members to go to his establishment. The operator then either runs the hostel or guest house stables himself or else employs qualified staff to do so.

Other organizations try and do it on the cheap by hiring the ponies, known as the "Pool" system, and employing local labour whether qualified or not. This means that the ponies may be out trekking all the week and have to return home varying distances for the week-end, only to return to the centre in order to go out again all the following week. And this with little or no feeding arrangements, badly shod and carrying hard, ill-fitting, often dangerous (to the rider) equipment, while the instruction and general organization is non-existent. Obviously an operator takes more interest if the animals belong to him!

N.B. The Ponies of Britain scheme is concerned only with the suitability, condition, treatment of the horses and ponies, their equipment and the elementary instruction provided at all trekking and riding holiday establishments, as distinct from purely instructional riding schools or small stables supplying hacking or hunting or livery facilities only. It is *not* concerned and cannot be held responsible for the accommodation or board of the riders at any centres, although at most on the approved list this is good, sometimes excellent. The Secretary is, however, prepared to reply to the various and numerous letters received asking for information—such as the following—when a stamped, addressed envelope is enclosed:

1. Whether or not an establishment is residential (R),

non-residential (N.R.), attached to hotel (A.H.), has nearby hotels and guest houses in which the riders are accommodated (N.H. and G.H.), lets out a caravan (C).

2. Type of country ridden over.

3. Type of horses/ponies used.

4. Whether the centre is suitable for young girls on their own. Trekking is *not* suitable for children under the age of 12, as there is no supervision after trekking hours.

5. Whether children are especially catered for, with a responsible housewife, or housekeeper, in charge at Riding Holiday Centres.

6. The suitability of any establishment's arrangements to the particular individual.

7. What sort of age groups are likely to be met with at any centre.

8. Whether the centre is gay, quiet, etc.

9. What other social or sporting activities are available.

10. Whether the experienced riders are catered for specially.

11. Whether novices are catered for specially.

12. Whether or not there is supervision of young people and children at all times.

The Ponies of Britain cannot be responsible for the accuracy of this information, which is constantly changing, nor can charges be given, as of course these fluctuate too. Riders should write direct to the centres and ask for current brochures.

Reception at Trekking Centres

Arrival. This is usually undertaken by the hotel or inn or hostel manager. Most centres ask you to arrive on the Saturday evening. Nothing happens that evening except possibly a short talk telling guests what the curriculum is for the morning, and/or simple instructions such as knot-tying.

N.B. Notes, information and "what to bring" notices, etc., are sent on booking.

Sunday Morning. Many centres hold a short service on Sunday morning; after this the trekking operator usually calls a meeting in some hut or large room when he takes down the names and addresses, occupations and previous experience of the guests (unless this has been given prior to arrival on the form provided).

Division into Groups. The guests are then divided into groups of preferably not more than eight and anyway not more than twelve, under an experienced person who can instruct, help and guide them across the country to be ridden over.

At many centres far too many riders are given to one instructor, which results in a muddle and in little or no opportunity for instruction.

Allocation of Ponies. The trekking operator and his head assistant should then allocate the ponies according to the experience of the trekkers. Instruction should then be given.

Simple Instructions. These should be as clear, correct and simple as possible and given by a qualified instructor:

1. They should be shown how to tie knots, i.e. the (non-slip) trekker's knot for tying up animals (see pages 28–30).

2. Where guests are expected to catch, groom, saddle, etc., their ponies, they should be shown where to find a halter, where the field is, which pony is theirs and how to approach it. How then to lead it, tie it up and groom it. This should never be permitted without supervision and so, with large numbers, this takes time.

3. How to place the saddle on the pony's back, how to fasten the girths, adjust stirrup irons, and how to place a headstall or bridle on its head.

    Some operators also allow the riders to place the bit in the animal's mouth, but this should never be done without instruction and under supervision. At others, only the operator or his staff are allowed to do this. To have novices fiddling about with their mouths tends to make the ponies difficult to bit and causes them to throw their heads up, and even to run back violently to evade the discomfort and real pain this may cause them. Where the bits are attached to the headstall "Ds" by a small strap it is obviously easier for novices to place the bit in the mouth, and also to drop it out again, than when they have to cope with the whole bridle. For this reason—and also because this type of headstall and bit make it so much easier to tie up and also to feed the ponies when on trek—this equipment is recommended above all other for trekking (see page 29).

4. How to mount, dismount, where to sit in the saddle, hold the reins and adjust the stirrup leathers. This is best done with the aid of a "dog-quiet" pony, but if because it is wet or for any other reason this has to take place indoors a wooden horse is very useful for demonstrating, and hooks on the wall do for bridle adjustments. Wooden horses as used in saddle rooms are easily and cheaply made. These activities will take the whole morning or more, dependent on the numbers being dealt with and their aptitude.

Sunday Afternoon and Monday Morning. Every trekker and every rider, of whatever experience, should then be asked to enter a school or an enclosed space and there perform some simple test, when it should be left to the discretion of the trekking operator or his head assistant to decide whether the mounts chosen for them are suitable or not.

Humans and animals both have their idiosyncrasies and quite a lot of chopping and changing may have to take place before the trekkers are allowed out of school. In the best centres none are allowed out on the mountains or moors until the trekking operator or his head assistant is satisfied that the ponies and their riders are happy and comfortable and that the novices have confidence in their mounts. Those with previous experience then go for a short trek while the inexperienced may remain for further instruction in the school.

Monday Afternoon. Either a very short trek or "break" on

Monday afternoons is arranged in some centres when the ponies or horses can have their feet attended to by the farrier in preparation for the week's work. This "break" is also probably welcomed by the riders before starting the serious trekking.

The "treks" then start; short distances of about five miles to begin with, increasing to not more than twenty-five miles in a day.

If your booking is for more than a week, you may go out trekking while the next arrivals are undergoing their initial training, or you may not. It depends on the centre.

Knowledge of the Countryside. Instructors should also know the nature of the country to be ridden over and what pitfalls to avoid; also its historical and romantic association, landmarks, etc. All this greatly adds to the interest.

They should know the whereabouts and how best to negotiate steep, stony mountain tracks, dangerous bogs, deep or treacherous fords, rickety bridges, sandy tracks, narrow gateways, low-lying branches, rabbit or other holes, dangerous main roads, and either warn or instruct riders or organize the rides to avoid these danger spots.

They should make it their business to contact the owners of the farms over whose land they wish to ride and obtain permission. Having done so, every care should be taken not to ride over new-sown grass or growing roots, gates should always be shut, and sheep and cattle left undisturbed. Shooting reserves should be avoided, especially in the nesting and shooting season.

One Person in Charge. One person should be in charge of the group and therefore responsible, but in many trekking and riding holiday centres, when the "boss" is not there in person, there is no one actually responsible. In some cases this is left to some local volunteer, when results are often most unsatisfactory and far from happy.

Intending trekkers and riding holiday-makers are well advised to make full inquiries regarding the "set-up" before booking.

Daily Information on Notice Board. A list of the groups arranged may be pinned up on a notice board, together with the names of the ponies allocated. This list is revised each morning by the trekking operator and/or his instructors to check for absentees. The ponies are looked over to see if they are well, sound and fit for work (e.g. they may have been kicked overnight or picked up a thorn or nail). Those animals found to have anything wrong with them will then not be taken out riding, their condition being attended to by the trekking manager or his staff.

This inspection is most important and should certainly not be the responsibility of the guests, but of the trekking operator or his staff.

Picnic Lunches. If guests are going out on an all-day trek, it is up to the trekking operator to inform the hotel or other caterers, so that picnic lunches are ready early in the morning.

Feeding Titbits. At many trekking centres the guests are encouraged to catch their own ponies. When doing this they should not offer the pony titbits. This may sound hard-hearted, but the reason for this advice is that if a pony always expects some titbit (and sugar is particularly in-advisable) they quickly get spoilt and snappy, and if the titbit is not forthcoming, sometimes quite vicious. If the ponies know that they are given a feed on being brought into the stables, only the most difficult will refuse to be caught, and these should be left to the instructors.

Because they cause ponies to become spoilt and snappy, titbits should only be given as a reward on coming in from work, or possibly in the evening when they have all been fed and can be given a titbit quietly, with no thought of catching them. The same applies to lunch-time. It is most unwise and unfair to the operators to allow your pony to share your lunch as they quickly become a perfect nuisance, and if denied food by the next rider can be quite unpleasant.

Catching Ponies

When approaching a pony in a field, walk up quietly to him and do not creep up from behind. Speak to him and, approaching his shoulder, pass the *loose end of the halter or headstall over and under his neck and form a loop by grasping the loose end under his neck before attempting to put on the head collar* (Fig. 1).

Your approach should always be quiet; never rush at horses and ponies, speak first and approach them so that

Fig. 1. Approach and technique for catching a pony

they can see you, *not* from behind. Give them a good pat but don't "tickle". If you have to take up a foot, place your hand on either the shoulder or the quarters and run your hand down the leg before you do so. When leading them walk by their shoulders and don't look back, like Lot's wife!

Midday Picnics

Spots for the midday rest periods and picnics should be carefully selected. They should have shade and water for the ponies and, if possible, posts, railings or trees to which the ponies can be attached, well apart from each other. This is especially necessary if they are fed with rations as they are jealous feeders, and therefore liable to kick and bite each other. A shed or stable is, of course, ideal but rare.

Fig. 2. Result of tying up a pony wrongly

Many centres graze their ponies only at midday. This is all right provided there is adequate space and grass, and the ponies do not run away! Good operators train their ponies so that, having removed their saddles and taken the bits out of their mouths, the ponies can be turned loose to graze without any fear of their straying or of being difficult to catch up again. This is the ideal method. Others tie the ponies to posts, trees, railing or even tufts of heather. Some hobble them by drawing the pony's nose level with its knees and attaching the end of the halter rope to one leg below the knee by means of a clove hitch, but only very experienced persons should do this, and only with animals who are accustomed to being thus controlled.

Some operators expect the rider to hold on to the pony while eating lunch. This is not a very good idea. The rider gets little relaxation, and the temptation to both to share the rider's lunch only teaches bad habits.

Provided there is adequate space and grazing and the ponies are trained not to move off, they can safely be left

Fig. 3. Sharing lunch

to graze and certainly this method eliminates the danger of kicking and biting; but all saddles must be removed or, when the ponies get down and roll—as they almost invariably do, especially if hot and sweaty—the saddle trees will inevitably be broken, which is both disastrous and expensive.

Tying up a Pony

No pony or horse should ever be tied up by anything attached to either a bit or bridle. If attached to a post by a bit, should the pony pull back, the pull comes on its mouth, which hurts it, so that the pony then panics and breaks away. This will also cause it to be nervous and afraid of further pain and so to try to get loose.

If attached to the bridle, the straps of which are much narrower and therefore weaker than a headstall, should the pony pull back it will break the strap and so get loose.

All animals should therefore be tied up either by the rope attached to the headstall or, better still, by the rope around its neck behind the ears, tied with a non-slip knot, the long end of which has been passed through the "D" or ring of the headstall under its chin and so to the post or rail to

Fig. 4. Tying up a pony correctly by rope round neck passed through "D" of headstall to immovable object, and tied with a non-slip, easily detachable knot, the bit being removed from the mouth

which it is tied with a *quick release* knot. Then if for any reason the animal tried to get free, most of the pull comes on its neck while still controlling its head. Fig. 4.

To tie a pony to a gate or rickety fence is obviously foolish as, should it struggle to get free, it may well carry the gate or fence with it, causing it to panic.

Some operators arrange the treks so that the midday rest takes place at some farm where stabling or rough sheds are available, so that the ponies can be tied up away from rain, hot sun and flies. This is, of course, ideal.

Simple Knots used on Treks and Riding Holidays

In well-run centres suitable knots for use when handling the ponies are taught to the riders by the trekking operator and his assistant. Those most in use are the Trekkers' knot, or

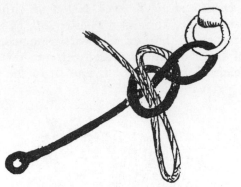

Fig. 5. Quick release knot

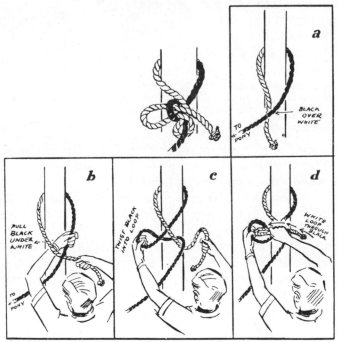

Fig. 6. Quick release non-slip trekker's knot

non-slip knot, the Hitch knot and the Clove Hitch; but any knot, provided it is perfectly secure and capable of being *rapidly undone*, is acceptable. (Figs. 5–6.)

When to let your Pony Drink

It is quite safe to let a pony drink at streams and rivers (but not stagnant ponds) when on "trek", but when proceeding at a faster pace, as may be the case on riding holidays, it is best not to allow it to have more than a mouthful or two during the ride. It should have its fill on return home.

All horses and ponies should have all they want to drink in the morning, but at least an hour before work and *before* being fed. The ideal is, of course, to have water always available whether in stable or field, but it is not always possible and water has to be given at specified times. Sometimes the old Army system of leading them to troughs has to be used through lack of labour and/or other better arrangements.

If a horse or pony returns very hot and exhausted in very cold weather, it is a wise precaution to take the chill off the water he has to drink.

Feeding of Ponies at Midday

Some establishments when out on trek, graze their ponies at midday, others arrange for rations to be available at some farm or other; at others, the trekkers carry rations in knapsacks attached to the saddle, when horsenuts, or better still Spiller's Horse and Pony Cubes are recommended, and are easy to carry.

If the animals concerned are otherwise well fed, to let them graze is adequate, but to tie them up in the hot sun with nothing to eat or drink, with the flies swarming round, while the trekkers enjoy themselves in the local inn is obviously wrong.

Snatching at Food on Trek

Allowing ponies to snatch at grass and trees, etc., or to stop and eat when on "trek" is also a most annoying habit, and even novices should try and check it by pulling the reins and speaking firmly. A pony that suddenly pulls the reins out of your hands may easily pull a novice rider right over its head!

Well-fed ponies should not require these extras, but it is admitted that it is very tempting to trekkers who are fond of animals to feed obviously under-fed ponies whenever they can.

Bring Your Animal in Cool

For the last half mile of the ride home it is reasonable and right to proceed slowly, or even to get off and walk. This especially applies to riding holidays, where the pace all day has been faster and the ponies, therefore, are liable to be hot and sweaty. Should they arrive home thus (which they should not) it is very much better to turn them straight out into the field, when they will have a roll, move about, dry off much more quickly and therefore not catch cold.

If, however, the animals concerned are stabled, their backs should be well patted after removal of saddles, to restore circulation, and either rubbed dry, which is hard work, or a rug should be thrown right over their backs (inside out), under which a good layer of straw should be laid along the spine. This aerates without causing chill, and when the sweat dries, it can then be removed with a good brushing (called strapping). The top door of the stable or box should be closed while the animal is drying off, to eliminate draughts.

Worries!

It is at centres where the animals involved are not properly fed, shod or treated, the equipment hard and "tatty", therefore sometimes dangerous, that the rider's enjoyment is marred by worrying about conditions. Increasingly, however, the public are beginning to recognize good from bad; they are learning not to believe all they are told and that endearing words used to a horse or pony do not mean necessarily that all is well. Only when the general public learn and have the courage of their convictions—when they refuse to get on animals that are, for various reasons, not fit to carry them—will these evils, such as we see daily in so many riding establishments, cease.

PLATES 1 and 2. A very important event—a pony being shod by a local farrier so that its feet are not bruised and broken on stony tracks.

PLATE 3. Trekkers at Rhayader, Powys, venture out to explore the unspoilt hills of mid-Wales.

PLATE 4. Ponies take advantage of the cool waters of the Wye, during a trek in mid-Wales.

No Worries!

In establishments and stables where the animals are obviously well, fit, cared for properly and reasonably treated and therefore happy, there is no need to worry and so spoil your holiday. Being hard and well they are less likely to sweat and so to have sores under the saddle or wounds on their legs; being well shod they will be all right on stony ground; and as they are fit they can work hard without distress.

Those that go out to grass by night can go straight out and have a roll (which to them is like a bath is to you) and having cooled off, can then be brought back into the stables for their evening feed of corn, bran and hay, to be turned out later in the cool of the evening when the flies have gone to bed.

The better fed they are, the less kicking there will be when they meet together in the field, and without flies to worry them they will soon either graze peacefully or lie down and sleep.

CHAPTER III

What to Wear and Other Practical Points

Jodhpurs or Slacks. Do not ride in cotton jeans. They look wrong and feel dreadful, especially on a long trek. They are, however, useful for work in stables. If you do not own or cannot afford a proper pair of well-fitting jodhpurs, then wear corduroy slacks or cavalry twill trousers; but jodhpurs not only give you a much firmer grip, they are much more comfortable and less likely to rub.

If breeches are taken then wear woolly stockings (as worn with plus-fours) and ordinary walking shoes, but these are very hot on a summer day. You cannot expect to have any grip, and therefore confidence, dressed in this material. You will feel much safer in something solid. Waterproof over-trousers such as golfers wear are excellent for putting over slacks or jodhpurs on wet days and are not expensive.

Underclothes. Suitable underclothes should be worn—those which will not ruffle up or wrinkle and so rub the wearer who may end by walking home. Nylon "frillies" or lace are most unsuitable and "Aertex" pants should be bought.

Long silk and wool or light wool under-pants reaching right down the legs are even less likely to ruffle or wrinkle and therefore rub the wearer, and are recommended for long days in the saddle, especially cold ones.

Footwear. Riding boots are useless for trekking, which invariably includes some walking, and are anyway only worn with riding breeches; jodhpur boots are correct, comfortable and prevent the ankles being rubbed by the stirrup irons, but they were originally invented for wear in a dry country (India) and are therefore not suitable in a wet one. A good strong pair of walking shoes with laces and well-defined heels are best and most practical, such as Highland Brogues; studs in the toes and heels only (so as not to interfere with the sole resting on the stirrup bar) are a help in mountainous country when trekkers frequently have to get off and walk.

Sandals, "casuals", and slippers are thoroughly inefficient, give no grip and are dangerous as they tend to slip through the stirrup irons. Slippers and house-shoes should be taken for indoor wear only.

Take a pair of Wellington boots, not only for catching ponies on a dewy or rainy morning and for stable work but also for riding in very wet weather or countryside, when they really are indispensable. They are not, of course, the thing for formal wear.

Be sure you have no buckles on your shoes or they may catch in the stirrup irons.

Macintoshes. A macintosh is essential, preferably a proper riding one or else a long gaberdine with a good wrap-over. Plastic ones, although light and convenient for carrying, tear very easily and *ponies can take fright if they billow out and flap in the wind (especially the cape type)*. Take good strong cord with you and roll the macintosh up tightly, place it over the front arch of the saddle and fasten securely.

Full length riding macintoshes are excellent but very expensive. Short waterproof ones are obtainable at firms supplying riding kit but, again, are expensive. Anoraks are better and cheaper, if possible worn with waterproof trews. Most good centres have a drying room.

Shirts. "Aertex" shirts or drip-dry cotton are ideal in summer and a light woolly jumper for colder days. Both are obtainable in various attractive colours. "Aertex" is light, porous, easy to wash and workmanlike, whereas nylon shirts and blouses in the circumstances look silly and are not cool.

Men and boys find zip-fastened jumpers or weatherproof jerkins are quite good and light, worn either with breeches and woollen stockings or with corduroy or cavalry twill slacks. Again, footwear with heels or boots are essential.

Headgear. It is wise to wear a hard hat out riding—either a bowler or a velvet hunting cap—as this acts as a protection when passing under low branches or should you fall, but bowlers would certainly cause a laugh in trekking centres; hunting caps are becoming and efficient.

Most trekkers, however, go out either bare-headed or in berets or scarves. On hot days this is understandable but on wet ones the hunting cap wins again. Failing this, something waterproof should be taken wrapped up inside your macintosh or in your pocket; and in your knapsack dark glasses as a protection to the eyes on sunny days—but they should fit securely and have plain, strong rims.

Take a scarf to protect the back of your neck on hot, sunny days from sunburn or sunstroke. In variable weather a light cardigan should also be taken, rolled up in your knapsack.

Leave your jewellery at home. Not only is there the danger of losing it, but it looks silly. The more simply you dress out riding the more comfortable and correct you will be. You will also look much nicer if your hair, if long, is tied back and covered with a net. Besides it is maddening to have it blowing in your eyes and face on a windy day, especially as you need to see what you are doing.

Rubbing, Sunburn, Insect Bites, etc. Remember to take talcum and dusting powder, and if you find that the saddle is rubbing you, smear wet soap over the part before you go out; do this before the skin breaks. Surgical spirit helps to harden the skin and so prevents rubbing.

If your seat bones are rather prominent and therefore not so well protected as some, it is a good idea to stick some "Elastoplast" on them, but this should be done while in a sitting posture, as if you were sitting in the saddle. If it is applied when in a standing position the "Elastoplast" pulls the skin when you sit down.

Take something for gnat and midge bites, and something for chapped lips. You will need calamine for sunburn, and some skin cream to put on before going out in wind and rain.

What to Wear on Riding Holidays

Much the same applies to riding holidays but cotton jeans are out of the question, except for stable work, and slacks are not recommended. It is really essential to have a well-fitting pair of jodhpurs with either jodhpur boots or strong walking shoes with well-defined heels, or breeches and riding boots.

A proper riding jacket will greatly add to your comfort and enjoyment.

Macintosh. A riding macintosh is again essential.

Footwear. Take Wellington boots for wet days—*not to ride in*, except possibly on very wet days or over boggy ground on informal occasions. Boots and shoes used for riding should have well-defined heels to prevent the foot slipping through the stirrup.

Riding boots (well-fitting and not too short) should be worn with riding breeches, or failing this long woollen stockings with good, strong lacing shoes. Or, of course, leather leggings can be used with breeches.

Jodhpur boots or strong walking shoes should be worn with jodhpurs or slacks or cavalry twill trousers.

Headgear. A hard hat—either a bowler or a velvet hunting cap should be worn and is a "must" when jumping.

Knapsacks. Provide yourself with a small, light knapsack, which must have strong straps or cord. Ex-U.S.A. respirator haversacks or Army surplus kitbags are strong and inexpensive. Some centres request you to carry these on your backs, others attach them to the "D" on the front of the saddle, where they tend to bump against your knees, unless again firmly strapped to the saddle (see Fig. 51). Which method is employed is largely a matter of taste. Some riders very sensibly carry their lunch in their riding coat pockets.

If your knapsack is slung over your back it is a good idea to have a piece of string attached to it which then passes around your waist; this keeps it from flapping about or

working forwards. Always keep a piece of cord somewhere
and a pocket knife.

Anything that flaps about is liable to frighten even the
quietest animal.

What to put in your Knapsack. Carry only essentials, i.e.
sandwiches, cake, fruit, etc., wrapped in polythene bags, a
plastic drinking bottle, never a glass one. A woolly jumper.
Glucose tablets, or sweets, will sustain you and take up little
room. If cameras are taken they should be as small and light
as possible.

Travel light and you will be glad you left out the extras
by the middle, let alone the end, of the day.

A Few Tips for Setting off on Trek

Naturally at all good establishments where there are qualified and experienced instructors, you will, as a beginner,
be taught the rudiments correctly. They may differ slightly
in their application from those given in this book or at other
good centres, but will fundamentally be much the same.

Your "Group" and Instructor/Guide. Having been allocated
to your group and instructor, you ask that instructor (or the
trekking operator) how then to proceed. There should not
be more than twelve riders at the most, preferably fewer, in
any one group. If you have friends with you, it can always
be arranged that they join your group unless for any reason
they wish to join another, i.e. more experienced riders.

Mounting. Ask to be shown the correct way to mount
(Fig. 7). If you have difficulty in getting up, use the mounting block which every centre should have, or anything else
solid which raises you off the ground slightly, such as a
large stone or a mound of grass. Bring your pony close up
to it, pick up your reins in the left hand and at the same time
grasp the pony's neck or lock of its mane. Stand facing his
tail but beside his left shoulder, place left foot in stirrup
iron (if you cannot reach it, let the leather strap down a hole
or two). Catch hold of the back of the saddle with the right
hand and give a little spring, swing right leg over the saddle
and lower seat gently into it. Do not thump down on it.

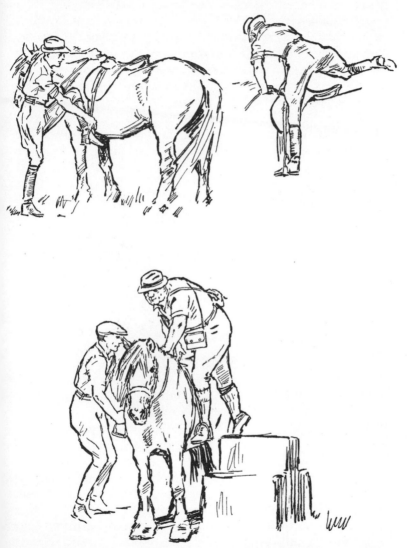

Fig. 7. How to mount—for the young and agile and for the not-so-agile

Get someone to pull on the right stirrup leather while you mount or the saddle will slew round with your weight, and you will have to dismount, undo the girths, replace the saddle in the proper position, and start all over again, or you may give your pony a sore back.

Dismounting. Take both feet out of the stirrups, lean forward, swing right leg over *backwards* and slip to ground (Fig. 8). Never keep one foot in the iron as if the pony moves you may be dragged. Never swing right leg forward over the pony's neck and so slide to the ground, or you may find yourself going over the pony's tail.

How to Move Off. Hold a rein in each hand. Each rein should pass round the *outside* of the hand OR between the little and third finger, and so across the palm of the hand

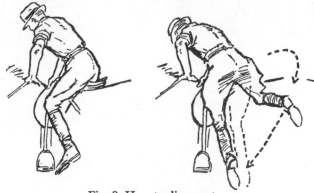

Fig. 8. How to dismount

and between the first finger and thumb. The fist should then be closed with the thumbs on the reins.

Give slightly with the hands to loose the pony's head, press hard or kick his sides with your heels, leaning slightly back, *not forward*.

Seat in the Saddle and Length of Stirrup Leathers. Do not be afraid to ask for help in mounting. Sit well down and straight in the centre of the saddle as near the front arch as possible, and with your seat well tucked under you—*not* stuck out behind. Your back should be straight and relaxed and shoulders nicely squared. Press your knees against the saddle flaps, and let your legs hang naturally, but with your heels well down. The instructor will then help you to adjust your stirrup leathers so that the tread of the stirrup irons knocks against your ankle joints. Then place your feet in the stirrup irons with heels well down.

Leathers that are too short cause the rider to sit at the back of the saddle like a jockey on a racecourse. But whereas a jockey stands up in his stirrups, you should not.

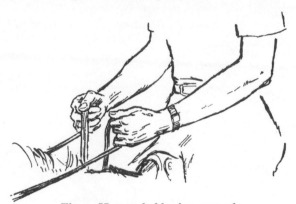

Fig. 9. How to hold reins correctly

Fig. 10. Leathers too long—leathers too short

Leathers that are too long cause the rider to drop his toes, give no support, cause loss of confidence and balance and, should the pony stumble, the rider may fall off. (Fig. 10.)

To adjust them yourself is easy—just follow the instructions given below.

To Lengthen Stirrup Leathers when Sitting in the Saddle. If, on mounting, you find your stirrup leathers are too short and therefore force you to sit on the back of your saddle, this is wrong and may injure your pony's back. To lengthen them, leave your foot in the iron, pull up the loose end of the stirrup leather, releasing the buckle from the hole it is in, then apply weight to the stirrup iron by pressing down with the heel of your foot, when the leather will automatically slide

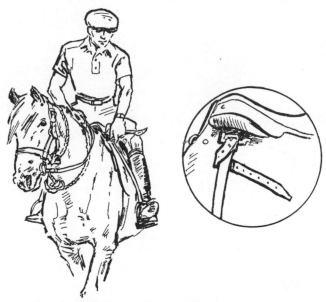

Fig. 11. Adjusting stirrup leathers without getting off or removing feet from irons

down and you can then insert the buckle into the hole in the leather which is most comfortable. Bear in mind that you must be sitting well down in the *centre* of the saddle, and that you must have your heels well down before finally deciding which hole is the correct length for you. Do the same with the other leather, then stand up in your irons, when you should just clear the arch of the saddle and *both* leathers should be of equal lengths. (Fig. 11.)

To Shorten Stirrup Leathers when Sitting in the Saddle. If, on mounting, you find yourself reaching for the stirrup irons and feeling somewhat insecure, it means that your stirrup leathers are too long. First of all, wriggle well down into the *centre* of the saddle, stick your knees into the saddle flap, put your heels down and while retaining your foot in the iron, take the height of it, and pull on the loose end of the leather, inserting the buckle in the hole which appears to give you the correct length. Do the same the other side, then stand up in the irons, ascertaining whether you then just clear the arch of the saddle, and that they are of equal length. The loose hanging end of the leather should then be tucked in the other two straps to keep it from flapping about or rubbing your legs.

A tip to help you to get the correct length of stirrup leather is to take your feet out of the stirrups when sitting well down in the centre of the saddle, when the treads of the irons should knock against your ankle joints.

N.B. If the bars of the saddle fit very close to the saddle flap, or the saddle itself is very new and stiff, it may be found difficult to insert the loop of the leathers behind them. Lifting the back of cantle of the saddle will make this a lot easier.

Tighten Girths. Make sure your girths are not too loose by asking the instructor, who will take them up if necessary.

Guiding your Pony. To go to the right pull gently on the right rein, give slightly with the left rein and press the pony's left flank with your left heel. Reverse the instructions when going to the left. (Fig. 12.)

N.B. Some ponies require to be kicked with the heel of the rider before they respond.

To Pull Your Pony Up. Press your knees into the saddle flaps, keep your heels well down into the stirrup irons, lean slightly back and pull on the reins saying, "Whoa" firmly. Do *NOT* lean far back. Relax pulls when pony responds. If he does not, relax, pull slightly and try again. (Fig. 13.)

The same applies to backing (i.e. moving backwards) an animal.

If you are a complete beginner, endeavour to keep your

pony in line with the others and try to keep up with the one in front. Listen to the group leader's instructions. It is unwise to get out of line unless you have some knowledge of how to guide and control your pony. This is particularly so going downhill, as if your pony gets out of line or falls behind he may decide to trot in order to catch up with the others, and to find yourself trotting downhill for the first time can be disconcerting. Trekking operators and instructors should organize each ride into groups with separate instructors so that the inexperienced riders are kept together when going down steep inclines.

Fig. 12. Guiding pony

If you are an experienced rider, you may well be capable of controlling your pony and even of proceeding at faster paces. But the person next in line to you may never have sat on a pony before and therefore it is up to you not to upset her or her pony and therefore to keep in line yourself. (See "Advice to Experienced Riders", page 48.)

Gates and Trees can Hurt. When going through a gate make sure you approach it in the middle and that it is open wide enough. Catching your kneecap on a gatepost or tree trunk hurts, and your pony will only look after himself and may forget you and your knees. The same applies to riding under trees. Your pony may be small enough to get under a branch which may remove you from the saddle. Passing under low branches, lean right forward along the side of your pony's neck.

Fig. 13. How to pull up correctly by leaning slightly back and applying legs. Also incorrectly by tipping forward and sticking out bottom, also exaggerated leaning back

Riding Down Steep Inclines. Be sure your girths have not worked loose or you may find yourself sitting up on your pony's neck like a monkey on a stick. Experienced riders maintain a central position but novices should lean slightly back and take a lock of the pony's mane in one hand or hang on to the neckstrap which, in all centres, should be provided for all novice riders (especially when learning to jump). Keep knees pressed against saddle flaps, heels well down and a firm contact on reins. (Fig. 14.)

Riding Uphill. When climbing very steep mountain tracks, lean well forward, try and remain in the centre of the saddle, and firmly grasp either the pony's mane or the *neck strap*, which is of great assistance not only to novices, but should

Fig. 14. Riding downhill

always be supplied to those learning to ride over obstacles. Do not at any pace hang on your reins—let your pony extend its neck to the full. A constant *light* feel should be maintained on the reins which should never be dragged at nor yet left dangling loose (Figs. 15–16.)

Midday Break—Removing Saddles. When it is time for lunch you should dismount, and at some centres the saddles are removed in case the pony gets down to roll and so cracks the iron inside it, which will be most uncomfortable for you and your pony, and a great expense to the operator. Ask the instructor how to lay your saddle down properly.

(Fig. 17.) Other centres may prefer you to leave the saddles on and tie the pony up, but in this case the girths should be loosened. This is entirely a decision for the instructor in charge. So much depends on the weather, location, etc.

At centres where ponies or horses are given extra rations

Fig. 15. Riding uphill correctly   Fig. 16. Riding uphill incorrectly

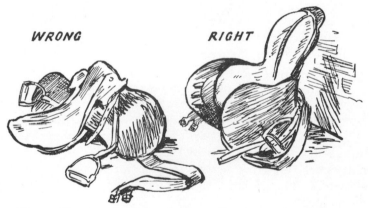

Fig. 17. Dressing and laying down saddle—incorrect and correct

at midday, watch out! In their natural state horses and ponies fight for food and they may do now, so be prepared for kicks and squeals. It is the duty of the trekking operator and his staff to make suitable arrangements and to see that this does not happen. To place the food on the ground in little heaps in close proximity, is asking for trouble. Hay and cubes should be placed in heaps, well apart, and ensuring there are more heaps than there are ponies. (Fig. 56.)

Crossing Streams and Rivers. Horses and ponies love water, especially on hot days. Not content with putting his head down to drink, yours may decide to have a bath, so if your horse or pony starts pawing the water and crouching down, kick his sides hard with your heels and pull his head up. If you cannot get him to move on, jump off, even if it means getting wet. Better this than getting rolled on as well.

It cools and freshens their legs to stand them in water, but watch they do not also lie down in it!

Riding on Roads and Leading a Pony. Keep well into the left-hand side of the road to allow for passing traffic, when riding. All trek leaders should instruct the trekkers to give way to traffic. If however, cars or lorries do slow down and give way, riders should always acknowledge this, by smiling and raising one hand, or even bowing the head. Not to do this invites drivers not to be so considerate next time. Nearly all treks have to go along roads at times and traffic is dangerous, and most car drivers are totally ignorant about the reactions of equines. A bird fluttering in a hedge, a dog rushing out or even a paper bag left in the gutter, cause even the quietest equine to shy.

To lead your pony, pass the reins over its head, take both in your right hand near the bit, carry the ends in your left. Do not look back.

Consideration for your Pony. If your pony stops, suddenly humps its back and raises its tail, the end of the world has not come. It merely wishes to pass water and should be allowed to do so, while you lean forward to take the weight off its loins.

Advice to Experienced Riders. If you have had previous experience and really can ride it is a good idea to find out before you go to a centre if more advanced trekking is provided for, when you may enjoy more freedom. This can usually be arranged, in the good centres, but do not say you can ride if you cannot (as many do!). Pride may have a fall. Even a trekking pony can have its moments!

PLATE 5. "I will lift up mine eyes unto the Hills from whence cometh my help." Looking down on Loch Awe with Ben Lomond in the distance.

PLATE 6. Away from the stress of town life, trekkers enjoy the companionship of co-operative native ponies while a competent Trek Leader points out landmarks, often of historic interest.

PLATE 7. Riding out along the sands at Polzeath in *Cornwall*. There is nothing better than salt water for horse's legs.

PLATE 8. Trekkers fording a river, with the Trek Leader in front. Note that his pony has on a rope halter, as do all the others, for tying them up during the lunch break.

Individual Attention: Beginners versus Experienced Riders. In some centres the organization is either non-existent or haphazard, which causes much dissatisfaction, since those who have never ridden before, who should be given individual attention, find themselves out trekking or riding with those who have had previous experience. The first may then be nervous and the second bored. It pays in the long run to have competent staff who can deal with both types.

Good staff can *make* an establishment especially if they are also good mixers, giving instruction in a friendly, helpful way and joining in the other social activities.

Rides and Treks always attended. Do not expect, even if experienced, to go out unattended. Not only do you not know the country and therefore where to ride, but in mountainous or boggy moorland country this can be dangerous not only to yourself but to your horse/pony. Any operator who allows a complete stranger to take his animals out on their own is wrong and extremely foolish. Riders have been known to ride hirelings literally to a standstill or to bring them in lame, etc. So do not expect any operator or owner to let you out alone until you are well known to him and he is satisfied you are capable and can be trusted, and that you know the country. Put yourself in his place.

Dismounting when Requested. Should your instructor ask you to dismount and lead your animal for any reason, i.e. to relieve the pressure on its back, to cross uncertain country or bridges, etc., do so without question as it is obviously for your own or the pony's good.

Flies. Do not at any time go into a pub or inn and leave your pony tied up without any protection from the sun and flies. Some trekkers think nothing of this. All good horsemen think first of their animals. (Fig. 18.)

Courtesy. Be friendly and polite to all farmers and landowners over whose land you may by courtesy be riding, also to local inhabitants. Apologize for any inconvenience or damage done; do not take things for granted. All land belongs to someone. It is very good of people to allow you to cross it. Make way for other traffic. Do not ride over farmers' hay or crops, and *shut gates behind you.*

Lighted Matches or Cigarette Ends. Do NOT throw cigarettes or lighted matches away regardless. Many serious forest or heath fires have been started in this manner.

Litter. Remember not to leave bottles and paper lying around after the midday picnic. Nothing so spoils the look of the countryside and annoys landowners. Be considerate of others.

Fig. 18. Inconsiderate riders: ponies outside an inn tied any old how to a rickety fence without shelter, food or water, with the saddles still on

How to Look After Yourself. If you have never ridden before, or not for a long time, treat yourself to a good hot bath immediately you come in, with a good handful of Epsom salts, or you will be very stiff the next morning.

For the same reason do not be persuaded to go for more than five miles the first day, and increase the distance gradually. The longest trek should not exceed twenty miles in a day. Remember that your pony has to take someone else out when you depart.

First Aid. At least one instructor and/or the trekking operator should carry a small first-aid kit and a hoof pick or "buffer" for removing stones from the animals' feet.

Give your pony a pat at the end of the day.

CHAPTER IV

General Advice to the Rider

PONIES and horses differ widely in nature and capabilities. To lump them all together is a mistake common to people who have never had much to do with them. They are like children in that they take advantage of fools, resent unfair, ignorant treatment, but respond to firm, kind handling. They are easily spoiled, never forget, but few are "born in sin". Any vice they may show, in nine cases out of ten, is due to mishandling or ill-treatment at the hands of man.

Some horses have more brains than others—all ponies are notoriously clever, even cunning, and are often the "bosses" if in a field with larger animals. All have muscles that tire, nerves that get on edge, lungs and hearts that wear out, teeth and heads which can ache. All feel pain to varying degrees, some more than others. Their memories are prodigious. They can find their way home by instinct, never forget somewhere they have been before, and remember ill-treatment of any kind.

Treat them badly and they react in different ways; some bear no resentment and suffer in silence; others fight back; some sulk, others just have their spirits broken. Treat them fairly, kindly but firmly, and they will respect you and give of their best. A patient trainer of horses and ponies gets the best out of them. A cruel one gets only what he forcibly takes out of them.

Don't expect them to work without food or water—no one can. Don't fill them up with food as you do a car with petrol! They have a digestive system which is easily upset.

If, when you approach him, your pony puts its ears back, there is a reason. He has been teased, ill-treated or, on the other hand, spoilt by too many titbits. But in good trekking and riding holiday centres, even complete beginners can rest assured that no harm will come to them. In well-run centres the animals are well treated, well fed and are therefore happy and placid, with bright eyes. In others you may find them under-fed and over-worked. They will look sad and dejected and have a dull, worried look in their eyes. Signs of ill-treatment are nervousness, starting, or afraid of having humans approach them or touch their heads.

Experienced people can tell at once whether a stable is a happy one or not.

Ponies and Horses Unsuitable for Trekking and Riding Holiday Centres

Work in trekking and riding holiday centres is hard. The animals in them are out of their stables long hours, often

Fig. 19. Unsuitable pony for trekking

with irregular, inadequate feeding; they travel long distances and, moreover, are often carrying novices, which is very much more tiring for them than if ridden by experienced persons. They often go out twice or three times a day. In trekking centres they are out all day climbing steep hills and descending them, which is even more tiring.

It is therefore impracticable to use either too small, lightly built, narrow-chested little ponies (except of course for children), or light-legged, thin-skinned "weedy" horses. One can only think that the reason some operators employ ponies that are much too small for their clients is that they are cheaper, and it is not so far for the riders to fall!

As a result, ponies aged no more than two or three years, which should not be working at all, with thin little legs and narrow, undeveloped bodies, are seen carrying heavy adults for sometimes as much as six hours a day, and moreover with sores under the saddle. This is not only very wrong for the pony but makes the rider look ridiculous. (Fig. 16).

N.B. By "too small" is meant 12 hands 2 inches and under (4 inches is a hand), the exceptions being the strong "cobby" types of ponies (see Fig. 27) which should, however, only be ridden by light adults and children.

"Too young" means any animal three years old and under and therefore not fully grown, still cutting teeth and therefore liable to digestive troubles, its bones not set and muscles still weak. Five years and over is the ideal age for this type of work. The exceptions are the very strong builds of native pony over this height which can be worked in their third and fourth year by experienced people for *short* periods.

Ponies and Horses Suitable for Trekking and Riding Holiday Centres

What is both practical and economical is any good, strong, quiet pony, cob or horse with an equable nature and a good constitution which is not easily upset and does not react too quickly to the rider's movements; and which is unafraid in traffic. They give confidence to the riders, they look right, can carry either light weights or heavy weights, and are economical to keep as they maintain condition more easily than do the other more delicate types (Fig. 20).

But riding holiday establishments, providing more advanced instruction, are recommended to have some horses which have more thoroughbred blood and are therefore more responsive, always provided they too have the right temperaments, and can be adequately fit and cared for to maintain good condition. Thoroughbreds require much more care and feeding than those less highly bred, which are therefore much more suitable for work of this description.

Children's Ponies. For children and small, light adults there are the smaller Welsh Mountain, Dartmoor and Exmoor ponies and those of unknown parentage of similar size and build (see Figs. 29, 30, 32). Some are very sturdy, and some small and light, especially a number being bred today. There are also the diminutive Shetlands, which are, however, only suitable for tiny tots.

Other Types of Pony that are also Suitable. There are innumerable "mongrel" horses and ponies of all types and sizes but of unknown parentage which are suitable by build and temperament for this exacting work, many of which come from Ireland. They are known as "general utility" horses and ponies, but the best ponies are native to these

Fig. 20. Suitable pony for trekking, fit and well shod

islands, having been bred here for centuries. These, in alphabetical order, are called Connemara, Dales, Dartmoor, Fells, Exmoor, Highland, New Forest, Shetland, Welsh (see Figs. 22–33).

How to Tell if a Pony is in Good Condition and therefore Fit to Work

SIGNS OF GOOD HARD CONDITION

1. Round, hard condition of neck, back and hindquarters, no bones showing at all.
2. Neck broad, firm and muscular.

3. Alert, head and tail up.
4. Bright eyes and contented, happy look.
5. Coat shining and skin loose.
6. Does not easily sweat and blow.

SIGNS OF GOOD SOFT CONDITION
   1. Fat but soft, large belly (because it is fed on grass),
      shining coat.
   2. Sweats and blows easily, and therefore galls easily.

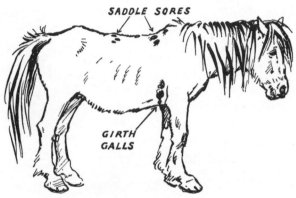

Fit. 21. Unfit pony, covered in sores and galls

How to Tell if a Pony or Horse is not in Good Condition and therefore not Fit to Work

SIGNS OF POOR CONDITION (Figs. 21, 53)
   1. Lean, skinny, bones showing, hip bones protruding;
      a groove running down the hind quarters by the tail.
   2. Neck, scraggy and thin; hard only because the bones
      of the neck can be felt, no muscle.
   3. Dull, dejected look, obviously unhappy. Worried look
      in eyes, and deep hollows above.
   4. Skin tight and coat "starey".
   5. Loses winter coat late in the summer instead of in the
      spring.
   6. Pendulous and large belly, indicating worms.
   7. Stumbles and knocks legs through weakness.

8. Blows and sweats under fast work.
9. May be lame through strains and sprains, or be afraid to put his feet to the ground because of painful joints, sore shins, or bruised soles or feet (Figs. 21, 48).

Lameness. An animal that is lame in its forelegs or feet nods its head at the trot and, if very painful, also at the walk. If lame in the hip, hind-leg or foot it "drops" on the sound leg to save the unsound, and again this is more noticeable at the trot than at the walk. Riders should look and see if a stone has become lodged in the hoof and report the lameness to the trekking operator or assistant. *No horse or pony should be worked if it is lame.* A horse/pony can go very "feelingly" without actually being lame (see above, 9).

Coughing. An animal which coughs slightly on first going out may merely be clearing its throat or lungs or have a slight cold or catarrh but one which coughs continuously and whose sides heave, or which makes a roaring noise when ridden fast, is broken-winded and unfit for work.

Colic. An animal which looks round at its stomach, paws the ground, and then gets down and rolls and groans, gets up and stands dejectedly and refuses food, and then gets down and rolls again has almost certainly got colic. The vet. should be sent for.

In Foal. No mare that is carrying a foal should have more than very light work (no galloping) for the first six months and should then *not* be worked at all. After the foal is born she again should not be asked to work for at least three months and then should not be allowed to get overheated while still feeding the foal.

Foals. Should not be weaned for at least five months, preferably six, if they are to be any good.

Both the mare and the foal when it is born should be well fed, on corn, bran, cod liver oil, mineral salts, etc., and not just hay alone.

Day of Rest. Every pony or horse in any centre should, if in full work, have at least one full day's rest per week.

The Age at which a Horse or Pony can be Worked. No horse or pony should be ridden consistently before it is four years old, although it should certainly be handled and broken in its third year. Over-riding and over-weighting of very young animals gives rise to strains to legs and back, sprains, damaged joints, and tends to ruin their natures through working them before their bones are set and their muscles strong enough. The reason for the increased riding of young ponies is, of course, because the sooner they work the sooner they earn money.

The exceptions are the heavier types, which, because of their strength, come to no harm if ridden in their third year for short periods by experienced people.

While four years is permissible in the stronger types of animal, five years and over is the ideal age for horses and ponies working in these centres. How long they can continue to work depends upon how well they are fed and cared for and therefore their condition and soundness.

One Way of Telling what Weight a Pony or Horse is Capable of Carrying without Strain. When a horse or pony is said to be "up to weight" one thing taken into account is the "amount of bone" it has. Bone is measured round the foreleg just below the knee.

An animal whose leg measures only five or six inches is "light of bone", which is too little and not fit to carry adults. Whereas 8 or 8½ inches is what is preferred in trekking centres.

Seven inches is average.

(*N.B.* To argue that racehorses are raced at two years old is beside the point. They are all born very early in the year and therefore get a six-months' start over other types; they are stabled and fed from birth and therefore mature early. They are then ridden by extremely light weights, always on a straight line over very short distances, in fact little further than they would normally gallop if loose in a paddock, and on soft, smooth surfaces.

CHAPTER V

The Nine Famous Native Breeds
of British Ponies

AT the Camping and Outdoor Life Exhibition, held at
Olympia, London, in January, 1960, the "Ponies of Britain"
were invited to stage a Trekking and Riding Holiday Ex-
hibit. It showed five British registered native ponies suitable
for this work and one unsuitable pony, together with the
correct and incorrect equipment. The interest created was
immense and the public asked so many questions about the
various breeds and their characteristics that a list of these
and their characteristics, origins and locations and present-
day usefulness is given here.

Not everyone knows that there are nine breeds of ponies
which have inhabited more or less the same territory for
centuries. They are, therefore, a national heritage and of
prime importance as foundation stock, being the basis of all
ponies and of a large proportion of horses as well. They have
the essential qualities of hardiness, stamina and intelligence.

Though not actually proved, it is highly probable that
these ponies' ancestors existed in Britain before man did.
But what is certain is that when the Celts came over to this
country they brought with them horses that were not pure
bred, but a cross between early prototypes of Arab (or
southern, warm-blooded) horses and those of northern (cold-
blooded) types. It can therefore be safely presumed that our
native pony stock is of Celtic (or European) origin and dates
back over 2,000 years. When the Romans came they brought
with them horses, acquired no doubt upon their African
campaigns, upon which to mount their legions. When they
returned to Rome they left these behind, thus vastly improv-
ing our native stock.

As the demand for lighter horses increased, native stock was used extensively, as it is today, as foundation stock. Mated with various types of blood, it provides animals of all sizes, endowing them with the "native" attributes of hardness, intelligence, courage, surefootedness and docility.

Luckily, however, throughout the years individual herds have remained safely tucked away in the wild mountains and moorland areas where, to this day, they can be found. Each breed has its own Society responsible for the breeding, registration and welfare of the breed, distributions of the premiums, etc. The demand for our ponies, both pure bred, native and upgraded, has never been greater. Trekkers will often see these ponies running out on the mountains and moors over which they ride—known as their "haunts".

The overseas markets are consistently increasing, especially in America and Canada, where they are very big dollar-earners. The home trade is also enormous as the public realize increasingly the virtues of our registered native ponies, and the fact that they are easier to keep than half-bred ones, such as part-bred Arabs and thoroughbreds, which, their blood being alien to this country, require additional attention and care in this variable climate. The small breeds have, of course, always been extremely popular and in demand as children's ponies.

Since the trekking and riding holiday movement started in these islands, the demand for the larger breeds exceeds the supply, for nothing can really hold a candle to our Highland, Fell, Dales, larger New Forest and Welsh Cob types of pony for work in mountainous country. Here, then, are the nine famous native breeds divided into large and small types—(a "hand" equals 4 inches and therefore an animal of 12.2 hands equals 50 inches, and an animal of 14.2 hands equals 58 inches.)

"LARGE TYPE" BREEDS OF NATIVE PONY

Connemara

Location. There is a wild mountainous district in Ireland loosely known as Connemara. The herbage is scant, the winds whistle, the bogs freeze in winter, while the Atlantic Ocean rollers dash themselves against the shores of Connaught on the west, and Galway Bay frames the land to the south. Yet here ponies have been bred and reared for centuries. It is said that four hundred years ago rich Galway merchants imported Arab horses, some of which escaped, as stallions do, to run wild upon the mountains among the native ponies, which may account for the fact that many Connemara ponies have definite Arab characteristics.

Height. Not exceeding 14.2 h.h.

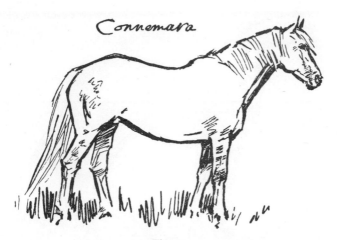

Connemara

Fig. 22

Colour. Grey, black, brown, dun, with or without black dorsal stripe, and roans and chestnuts, although these are rare; yellow duns or golden with white manes and tails (now called Palomino) are quite common and popular.

Characteristics. Free, easy action with sloping shoulders and excellent temperaments. Good jumpers and hunters.

Usefulness. Excellent for use at riding holiday establishments; equally good for adult or child, but at present hard to come by.

Secretary: Mrs. J. A. F. Barthorp, English Connemara Pony Society, The Quinta, Bentley, Farnham, Surrey.

Dales

Location. Natives of the North Yorkshire dales and Co. Durham.

Height. Not exceeding 14.2 h.h.

Colour. Dark brown (known as "heckleberry"), black, bay, occasionally grey—only very slight white markings accepted as typical.

Characteristics. Smart, stalwart appearance, strong and very active, with profuse manes and tails which must be straight and not curly, and "feathers" at their heels, all of

Fig. 23

which are Nature's protection from the weather. Great bone and good, hard, open feet; docile and clever; up to weight and economic to maintain.

Usefulness. Have carried—and still do—North Country farmers out shepherding on the grasslands of northern England for centuries; they are returning to popularity along with the trekking movement, for which they are excellent. They are first cousins to the Fells.

Secretary: G. Hodgson, Esq., Dales Pony Society, Ivy House Farm, Hilton, Yarm-on-Tees, Yorks.

Fells

Location. Cumberland, Westmorland, and the northern end of the Pennine range—1,300 feet above the sea-level.

Origin. The same as the Dales but run very much truer to type. In old days they carried lead ore from the mines in the hills to the seaports, as well as other merchandise. They were, and still are, used extensively for general utility purposes on the grassland farms of northern England as from time immemorial.

Height. 12.2 h.h. to 14 h.h., not more.

Colour. Black predominates, and ponies run so true to

Fig. 24

type that it is difficult to distinguish between them. There are also browns, greys and occasional bays. Broken colours do not exist in true-bred ponies and white markings are not acceptable for the Stud Book.

Characteristics. Good length of rein, slightly low-set tail, rather long in the back, fine silky hair on mane and tail, which must not curl, and open, hard feet. Delightful temperament, easy to break, handle and maintain.

Usefulness. An excellent riding pony for adult or child, and another breed that is ideal for trekking and riding holidays. They are not only surefooted and docile, but are also good jumpers and hunters. This breed is under Royal patronage, as the Royal Family have driven their own Fell pony,

"Windsor Gipsy", to win the Harness Class at the Royal Windsor Horse Show.

Secretary: Miss P. Crossland, Fell Pony Society, The Packway, Windermere, Cumbria.

Highlands

Location. The Scottish mainland and the Western Isles, now also in many studs in the South.

Origin. It is possible that ancestors of these ponies inhabited Britain before the Ice Age. There are two types:

1. The pure pedigree Highland pony.

Fig. 25

2. The heavier type which has probably had infusions of cart-horse blood at one time. Native ponies derive from two famous strains. Atholl strain, belonging to the Duke of Atholl at Blair Castle, Perthshire (ponies from which he lends to the Tilt and Killiecrankie Hotels, Blair Atholl, for trekking), and the Rosebaugh strain. Both descend from two famous stallions, Herd Laddie and Bonnie Laddie.

Height.

1. Pure-bred pony of small type, 13 h.h.–14 h.h.
2. Larger types, sometimes called "garrons", up to 14.2 h.h.

Colour. Very varied, but grey predominates. Dun, especially with zebra markings on forelegs and thigh and a black dorsal stripe along back and across the shoulders, are very characteristic. Also silver duns with black markings, browns, occasionally bays, but no broken colours permitted, and only very slight white markings which may denote crossings by Clydesdale blood, which is greatly discouraged.

Characteristics. The mane and tail and slight "feathers" on the legs must be straight and silky. Extremely good and open feet; immensely powerful quarters and loins in order to carry heavy weights up steep mountains with ease. This breed is also under Royal patronage, ever since the days when Queen Victoria rode and drove out at Balmoral using them and the late King Edward VII rode his famous pony, Jock.

Usefulness. A "no trouble" pony, capable of doing any job. Ridden for centuries by their owners and also used for carrying game and stags from hill or forest. When schooled, make excellent riding ponies for adult or child, and are naturally good jumpers. Are invaluable for trekking, being the most famous pony of all; easy to feed, handle and maintain and very sure-footed and docile.

Secretary: D. M. Patterson, Esq., The Highland Pony Society, 8 Whinfield Road, Montrose, Angus.

New Forest

Location. The New Forest, Hampshire.

Origin. Mentioned in the Charters of King Canute, but have experienced, more than any other breed, various experiments in breeding, which has made them less typical than any of the other breeds.

Height. 12 h.h.–14 h.h.

Colour. Any colour but piebald and skewbald, which are not accepted in the Stud Book.

Characteristics. Lighter of bone than the other large breeds owing to the lack of protein in the grazing, under the trees in the Forest. Have improved tremendously over the last ten years in quality, conformation and performance, and if well fed from birth develop into large and splendid ponies.

Usefulness. Probably the best general-utility riding pony of all. Generous and honest, naturally good jumpers, with staying power, and immensely popular all over the country for both adults and children. Excellent for riding holiday purposes; small ones for children and the larger ones for both children and adults. Almost always traffic-proof, owing to the proximity of the roads to the Forest.

N.B. It is not a kindness to stop cars and feed ponies that wander by the roadside, as this only encourages them to frequent the highways where hundreds are killed and injured every year. It is also highly dangerous to fast-moving traffic.

Fig. 26

Secretary: Miss D. Macnair, New Forest Pony Breeding and Cattle Society, Beacon Corner, Burley, Ringwood, Hants.

Welsh—General

These ponies come under a general heading of "Welsh" as all types of Welsh cobs and ponies derive from the original Welsh Mountain Ponies. There are four divisions in the Welsh Stud Book namely, Welsh Mountain ponies (Section A) which are the original small ponies of 12 h.h. and under; Welsh ponies (Section B) which are either Welsh mountain ones which have grown over 12 h.h. or those upgraded by a varied infusion of T.B. and/or Arab blood to obtain the height of not exceeding 13.2 h.h.; Welsh ponies of Cob type (Section C)—again ponies which have gone over the height limit of Section A or have been purposely bred larger and stronger by infusions of other blood; Welsh Cobs (Section D) with no height limit but usually not exceeding 15 h.h.

Welsh Ponies of Cob Type. *(Registered in Section C of the Welsh Stud Book.)*
These come under the heading of "large type" ponies.

Location. All over Wales and also in England, Scotland, Ireland and increasingly overseas.

Origin. Bred from the original smaller Welsh Mountain native ponies crossed with various other types to get more bone substance and height.

Height. Not exceeding 13.2 h.h. if they are to be registered but many of the best are over this and around 14–14.2 h.h.

Colour. Greys predominate but bays, browns, chestnuts, blacks, cream duns are all common; piebald and skewbald are not accepted as pure bred but many of this type are "broken" coloured and none the worse for it! For example see the gipsy ponies grazing by the road-side or pulling caravans, many of these ponies being great types.

Characteristics and Usefulness. The best possible general utility ponies, with usually quiet, even temperaments and a certain amount of quality about them. Alert, active, intelligent and immensely strong and sure-footed, they are increasingly being used in trekking centres, and have always been popular in riding ones generally.

Secretary: (See under "Welsh Mountain Ponies", page 75).

Welsh Cobs. *(Registered in Section D of the Welsh Stud Book.)*

Location. At one time bred all over Wales and extensively used both for riding and driving. Now less so, but also bred in England and Scotland.

Origin. Derived from the Welsh Mountain ponies interbred with larger types such as Hackney, Roadsters and other larger blood.

Welsh Pony of Cob Type
(Section C)

Fig. 27

Welsh C
(Section

Fig. 28

Height. No height limit but 15 h.h. is the unofficial law.

Colour. Greys, chestnut which predominates, roan, cream, dun, black, bay, brown, but broken colours not acceptable for registration though many good animals have this colouring.

Characteristics. Very smart, stylish appearance and action, small alert heads and large kind eyes, good tail carriage—always docked until the law forbade this. Strong, docile, very sure-footed and hard, with instinctive knowledge of the country and of mountains.

Usefulness. Wonderful animals, good for all purposes, either ridden or driven. Used extensively in light trade vehicles and coster carts when they won most of the prizes! They are coming into their own again, not just as trekking animals but as show jumpers and hunters as they are mostly great performers over fences. They are therefore good foundation stock for breeding show jumpers and utility hunters and animals of all kinds.

Secretary: (See under "Welsh Mountain Ponies", page 75).

General. Because of the nature of the country ridden over, especially the steep mountains of Wales and Scotland, the rolling grasslands of northern England and the moors of the West Country, no more suitable animals can be found than the above "types" for both trekking and riding holidays of all descriptions. They all have an instinctive knowledge of rough "trappy" country, and seldom stumble or fall under the most severe conditions where other types would prove useless.

Do not think because they are heavier than the horses and ponies you have previously ridden or are accustomed to see at shows, etc., or because they have "feathers" on their legs, that you are being asked to ride carthorses! The hair on their heels is Nature's protection against wet and weather as it prevents the water getting into the hollow of their heels and causing cracks like chilblains. They need all their strength to carry you safely up and down steep, stony mountains and over deep, boulder-ridden streams. In other words, "each man to his trade".

You will also find, however, if you go on a riding holiday

and wish to go at faster paces, that they can gallop and jump with the best.

"SMALLER TYPE" BREEDS OF NATIVE PONY

The following describes the smaller breeds of our native ponies which are world-famous and fetch large prices, sometimes reaching four figures, at home and overseas.

Dartmoor

Location. Moorland country of roughly 122,000 acres between the English Channel on the south and the Atlantic Ocean on the north, known as Dartmoor, where the altitude in parts is 1,000–2,000 feet above sea-level.

Origin. Dates back over two thousand years.

Fig. 29

Height. Must not exceed 12.2 h.h.; pure-bred ponies rarely exceed 11.2 h.h.

Colour. No colour bar except piebald and skewbald, but white markings frowned upon.

Characteristics. Small "pony" heads with very small ears, straight, low, smooth paces. A tendency to rather long "dipped" back, but the whole appearance like a miniature "thoroughbred". Possibly the best children's ponies of all the breeds because of their smooth action and wonderful temperaments. Not suitable for carrying adults.

Secretary: D. W. J. O'Brien, Esq., Dartmoor Pony Society, Chelwood Farm, Nutley, Uckfield, Sussex.

Exmoor

Location. The moors in Somerset known as the Forest of Exmoor.

Origin. The Exmoor Society claims that its ponies closely resemble the European wild horse which spread northwards in prehistoric times from the Caucasus Mountains. Certainly one of the oldest breeds and one which has remained most typical. It was these ponies that so impressed the Romans when whirling the war chariots into battle that they took numbers back with them to Rome.

Height. 12.2 h.h. for mares, 12.3 h.h. for stallions.

Fig. 30

Colour. Brown, bay and dun. No white markings allowed anywhere.

Characteristics. Very marked in this breed and include mealy-coloured muzzle, large full eyes set in a broad brow, known locally as "toad" eye, and coats which differ in texture from any other breed, resembling that of deer in winter, being harsh, springy and close, and therefore impervious to wind and rain, while in summer they shine like brass. Possibly the toughest of all the breeds.

Usefulness. Wonderful ponies for experienced children and small, light-weight adults, but a bit too high-couraged for novices. Admittedly they have carried their farmer-owners over Exmoor for centuries, but the ponies bred then had more bone and substance than those being bred today, the majority of which are not suitable for carrying heavy adults for long hours. Because something has been done for years it does not necessarily mean it is right! First-class foundation stock for breeding larger ponies endowed with stamina, soundness and performance. This breed is in great demand overseas and in the north of England.

Secretary: R. G. Gibbins, Esq., Exmoor Pony Society, Park House, West Porlock, Somerset.

Fig. 31

Shetland

Location. Orkney and Shetland Islands in the north of Scotland. Now bred all over the country and overseas.

Origin. Said to be the oldest breed, some think of prehistoric origin. The smallest of all the breeds and for centuries the only means of transport in the islands of their origin where they carried all goods, fertilizers such as seaweed, and also probably their owners!

Height. From 37 inches to 42 inches.

Colour. Any colour including broken ones.

Characteristics. Immense strength and bone for their size.

Very lively and rather headstrong. Look like woolly bears in winter-time but have satin coats in summer. Excellent in harness as they can trot fast and far and are untireable.

Usefulness. Still fulfil their original purpose on their native islands. Good children's ponies (tiny tots) provided they are properly handled and broken and not treated like large dogs. Very popular as pets at home; also overseas, especially in U.S.A., where they are crossed with hackney blood to produce harness ponies.

Secretary: D. M. Patterson, Esq., The Shetland Pony Stud-Book Society, 8 Whinfield Road, Montrose, Angus.

Welsh Mountain

Registered in Section A of the Welsh Stud Book—the original native pony.

Location. The Welsh Mountains all over Wales, and in studs in this country, Scotland, and all over the world, especially in America, and Canada.

Origin. They are the foundation stock of all Welsh ponies and cobs. Extensive mating with thoroughbred and Arab blood also produces larger high-class animals. Almost certainly of Celtic origin, probably derived from Roman pack-horses, themselves derived from the Romans' African campaigns. Arab thoroughbred and other blood has been used throughout the centuries, although the improvement within recent times has been mainly achieved (and rightly), by selective breeding inside the breed itself.

Height. 12 h.h. maximum.

Colour. All colours, except piebald and skewbald which are not eligible for registration. Heavy white markings not encouraged, but wall or silver eyes not uncommon and permitted.

Characteristics. Much in common with Arabs, especially about the head which should be fine, full of quality, with full, dark eyes and a slightly dished muzzle. Neat, small ears held pricked and a gay head and tail carriage. Fine and profuse mane and tail. The whole appearance full of "personality" (or "presence" as it is called in the show world).

Usefulness. First-class ponies in every way, the most universally popular of all the breeds and therefore expensive. Good children's show and utility ponies and also excellent in harness. They are, of course, *not* suitable for carrying

Welsh Mountain Pony
(Section A)

Fig. 32

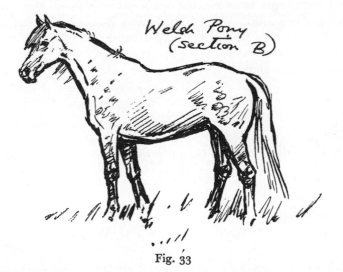

Welsh Pony
(section B)

Fig. 33

adults. Enormous overseas market, especially in America and Canada where they are big dollar earners.

Secretary: T. Roberts, Esq., Welsh Pony and Cob Society, 6 Chalybeate Street, Aberystwyth, Dyfed, Wales SY23 1HS.

Welsh Ponies

Registered in Section B of the Welsh Stud Book.

Location. Everywhere.

Origin. Bred up from the Welsh Mountain pony, either pure-bred that have outgrown the height limit of 12 h.h. or those with infusions of thoroughbred Arab and other blood.

Height. From 12 h.h. up to 13.2 h.h.

Colour. As above.

Characteristics. Very similar to the Welsh Mountain, only larger.

Usefulness. First-class riding ponies, very popular at shows, and suitable in every way for children and light adults. The lightly-built ones are extensively used in the Pony Club for children and those more strongly built and around 13 h.h. or 13.2 h.h., being both sure-footed and sagacious, are good for riding holidays as they have easy paces and jump well. The stronger, heavier ones *can* be used for trekking, carrying light or medium weights, but those of cob type are better for this job.

Secretary: (See under "Welsh Mountain Ponies", page 75).

CHAPTER VI

Equipment

Saddles—from the Rider's Point of View

NOTHING is more uncomfortable or more likely to rub the seat and legs of the trekker than sitting on a hard, ill-fitting saddle for long hours at a time. A bad saddle can completely mar a good ride.

Guests at trekking centres should expect to find the leather of the saddles they are provided with soft and supple; this includes the saddle flaps and the straps to which the girths

A WELL-FITTING SADDLE

SADDLE PRESSING ON PONY'S SPINE

Fig. 34   Fig. 35

are attached and the stirrup leathers, lest they break and cause an accident. The saddle should be well stuffed to enable the rider to sit in the centre and not be tilted either forwards or backwards. *The front arch should clear the pony's shoulders by two fingers' breadth* **when the rider's weight is in the saddle.** If it is found that either the arch at the back or that at the front of the saddle is pressing down on the bones of the animal's spine or shoulder, then *as a temporary measure only* a thick (Army) blanket, a felt "numnah", or a sheep-skin, should be placed under the whole saddle, or a thick knitted pad should be placed under the front arch to raise it off the pony's spine until the saddle can be re-stuffed. Silly little bits of material under saddles only make matters worse.

The trekking operator should be told if for any reason a rider is not comfortable, or if the hard frame of the saddle rests at any point of the pony's spine. There should be an air passage through the saddle from front to back *when the rider's weight is in the saddle.*

New Saddles. The stuffing of saddles, especially of new ones, tends to sink very rapidly, and they need re-stuffing within quite a short time of being bought if they are not going to cause sores on the animals; do not imagine that because a saddle is brand new it must fit.

All saddle linings naturally collect grease and sweat, and unless regularly cleaned cause more sores than they prevent. (Saddle cloths can be used to keep linings clean—these are more easily washed.)

Saddles—from the Horse's or Pony's Point of View

It has been proved that on the whole the best kind of saddle for trekking is the ordinary hunting one, provided it fits the animal (Fig. 36). Every pony should have his own saddle fitted specially, and this should be hung up in the saddle-room under his name, together with his other equipment.

A saddle in which the iron bar of the front arch (which lies inside it and passes down both sides of the animal's shoulders) is too wide, will roll about. Those with the iron arch too narrow will pinch the animal. Saddles should fit the animal as well as the rider, *but the animal is the more important.*

Army Saddles

These obviously must have their advantages or they would not have been used by the Army under all sorts of conditions for very many years and especially in mountainous country. They have also been tried out trekking but without marked success, largely because, having originally been made for full-sized horses, they are much too heavy, weighing as they do 19 lb. or over without fittings or rider, and are also far too long and big for ponies. Their use on very small ponies is to be deplored, because they reach much too far back—and so rest upon the loin instead of the centre of the back—and too far forward—so interfering with the free movement of the shoulder blades. As the kidneys lie under the loin, this is obviously not a good thing; the less weight on any animal's loin the better. Some argue that because these saddles have dipped seats, it is not possible for the rider to sit on the back of the saddle, but to begin with they are so large that if placed on a small pony the weight of the rider is anyway in the wrong place, and should he—as he can—sit back on the seat, the damage done is worse than if he did so in an ordinary hunting saddle.

Fig. 36. Hunting saddle   Fig. 37. Army saddle

The Iron Arch Universal Military Saddle now used (fitted with felt pads as always), is smaller and measures $17\frac{1}{2}$ in. from front arch to back. It is therefore lighter and can be used with a plain brown Army blanket, which is very much better than other more flimsy material, provided—like everything else—it is kept clean and free from sweat crystals and grease. But even if its weight could be brought down to that of the hunting saddle, which is about 14 lb., the latter is still considered the best for trekking and of course for riding holidays. For post-trekking the Army-type saddle has of course the advantage of a number of "Ds" for attaching packs, etc., and also—should the animal's back show signs of blistering or rawness—the blanket can be folded to remove pressure at that point. (For notes on Post-Trekking, see page 111.)

But, by and large, there is nothing to touch the ordinary English hunting saddle.

American (Cowboy) Saddles

These require a different technique and seat, but are very comfortable to those who are accustomed to them. In them the rider rides with a straight leg. They are good on a horse's back because the rider must sit right down and in the centre of the back. They are very decorative but they weigh at least 30 lb., are very expensive, and are unsuitable for ponies.

Fig. 38. Saddle worn and needing re-stuffing

Blankets, Pads, etc., placed under Saddles

A number of blankets or pads or other bits of material in a saddle-room is a sure sign of inefficiency and that the saddles need re-padding. Some animals, however, do require a saddle cloth under their saddles, especially for long-distance riding. Sheepskin (with the wool next to the animal's skin) is best but expensive. Felt "numnahs" can be used but are not comparable to sheepskin, real or simulated. Plastic foam mats are not satisfactory.

Also, as a *temporary* measure, or because a new pony has arrived for which no saddle has yet been obtained, some form of padding may be necessary. In this case a thick Army blanket (folded carefully with no wrinkles and so placed to relieve pressure where needed); or real or simulated sheep-skin made of man-made fibre are best, and easy to clean, but require to be washed and dried or they will become greasy and sweaty and cause sore and blistered backs. The bother and expense of trying to cure sore backs with useless ointment are endless. The only real cure is to stop working the animal until the back is completely healed.

Why Horses and Ponies get Sore Backs, and Where

The chief reasons for a pony/horse getting a sore back or an abscess are:

1. That the animal is not fit or too thin. Those fed on grass only are soft. They therefore gall easily and should be brought into work gradually and not suddenly. Those not sufficiently fed, and therefore too thin and lacking muscle, get sores more easily than those which are well fed on corn (Fig. 21).

2. Friction, i.e. when a saddle keeps moving because it does not fit properly or the rider rolls—movement caused going up and down or over rough ground at fast paces.

3. Pressure continuously on one spot, which stops the blood circulating and so causes dead skin. (It is for this reason that considerate trekking operators sometimes ask riders to get off and walk as this relieves the pressure on the backs of the ponies, thus allowing the blood to circulate again.)
   N.B. The skin on the backs should be hardened before the season starts by applying either a strong solution of salt and water or methylated spirits; but *not* when the skin is already broken.

4. Warble Flies. Lumps may appear on the pony in spring and early summer, caused by warble flies laying their eggs the previous summer. The lumps are maggots, and if situated under the saddle, trouble is likely, especially as the warmth of the saddle makes the maggots hatch out more quickly.

PLATE 9. Highland ponies from Blair Castle Trekking Centre setting out for a day's trek. The ponies are also used by trekkers from the Killiecrankie and Tilt Hotels.

PLATE 10. Trekkers starting out on a day trek complete with saddle bags holding food for the ponies and sandwiches for the riders, to be enjoyed during a mid-day halt.

PLATE 11. Typical of the type of beautiful hill country which can be enjoyed by trekkers of all ages over 12 years. (It is better for young children of 12 years and under to go to a Riding Holiday Centre where there is instruction and supervision at all times.)

(*Treatment:* apply moistened derris root to encourage the maggot to ripen, and, when a small hole appears, squeeze the lump with both thumbs, when the maggot will pop out. Dress with diluted T.C.P. or dust with sulphanilamide powder.)

Fig. 39. Girthing up correctly

How to Place the Saddle on the Animal's Back

Pick up the saddle already "dressed" (this means that the stirrup irons should be pulled up as described on page 109). Lift and place on the animal's back very well forward, and slide back into position in the *centre* of the back behind the shoulders. This movement lays the hair in the right direction.

Fastening Girths

The two buckles of the girth are attached (usually but not always) to the first and third straps under the right-hand saddle flap. The girths are then passed underneath the pony and attached to buckles on the left-hand flap of the saddle. To tighten, place the head under the saddle flap to keep it out of the way, take hold of one strap at a time, and, bending the knees, heave upwards gently and gradually, inserting the tag in the hole of the strap where you are able to make it meet. Do the same to the second buckle and third strap.

While a girth is being fastened the animal frequently blows itself out with air to prevent the girth being too tight. Later it deflates, when the girth may be too loose. All riders, therefore, look to their girths before moving off and the trekking operator or staff should then be asked to take the girth up a hole or two if necessary.

There should be no wrinkled skin under a girth when correctly adjusted. Riders should be shown how to avoid this by passing a hand behind the girth to smooth the skin.

On dismounting, girths should be loosened. No animal should be left for any length of time without this thought for its comfort.

Care of Stirrup Leathers

It is dangerous to ride with stirrup leathers, which, through lack of saddle soap or Koa-chalin, white "Vaseline", etc., have become hard and therefore brittle. A broken strap going downhill, even at a walk, can cause an accident. Guests have every right to look and see if the leather of their equipment is soft and supple and therefore safe.

Reins

The same applies to reins. If these break, or the buckle which fastens them together gets broken and the reins separate, the rider may find himself in trouble.

Stirrup Irons

These should be wide enough ($\frac{1}{2}$ inch either side of foot) easily to admit the rider's feet. Small, narrow irons, and on the other hand over-large ones, are a great danger because if the rider should fall off a foot may get caught in the iron, and being unable to get free he will then be dragged along the ground.

In the best riding holiday establishments children are provided with safety irons.

Suitable Bridles for use in Trekking Centres

The most practical equipment for ponies in trekking centres

Fig. 40. The best kind of trekking bridle, bit and rope

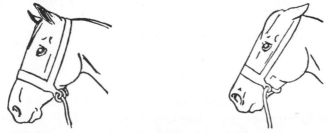

Fig. 41. Halter, correctly adjusted with knot under chin, and incorrectly with no knot tied

is a leather headstall with a snaffle bit (preferably what is called the half-moon snaffle) attached by small straps to the metal "D" at the side of the headstall. A single rein is then attached to the ring of the bit. Brow bands should be dispensed with as they tend to rub the base of the ears; while too narrow bits rub the corners by the mouth (Fig. 44).

In some establishments a strong rope is attached to the "D" of the headstall *under the pony's chin*. In others, the rope is first placed round the pony's neck just behind the ears and tied with a non-slip knot. The long end is then passed through the "D" under the pony's chin, and when on trek is again passed around the pony's neck, only lower down and tied at its chest in another non-slip knot (Fig. 40). Some organizers use bridles and bits, and place rope halters beneath them. This is not nearly so satisfactory as very strong leather headstalls and ropes.

Suitable Bridles and Bits for Riding Holidays

In riding holiday establishments the bits vary, but the only one for novices is the snaffle (Fig. 42). Young ponies, too, should have nothing else placed in their mouths for a year or more. Severe bits and curb chains are not for novice riders or young animals, and should not be given them.

Plain jointed snaffle   *Half moon*

Fig. 42. Snaffle bits

Neckstraps. The neckstrap of a martingale or some other strap or stout piece of string round a horse or pony's neck is most useful to novice riders and children and indeed at times to everyone, even the most experienced, to hold on to by the fingers of one hand. Those who use them should never be ridiculed. It is far better to hold on to a neckstrap when learning to jump or going up and down steep hills, and generally learning to ride, than to jab the animal's mouth and therefore both to pain and disappoint it (Fig. 43).

Girths. These are the straps which hold the saddle in place, and are attached by buckles to short straps under the leather flaps on either side of the saddle under the rider's knees. Girths should be first attached to the right-hand side of the saddle, passed under the pony and attached to the straps on the left side. Girths of whatever material should be kept in good repair or riders may suddenly find themselves on the ground.

They can be made of leather, string, nylon, webbing or lampwick.

Fig. 43. Neckstrap in use

Fig. 44. Badly-fitting, too small bridle causing sores

Lampwick. Lampwick has been proved the best for trekking centres. It is easy to clean, does not cause sores, does not stretch or shrink, and is well worth the extra expense.

A girth made of this should be tubular and about four inches wide with two buckles at each end.

String Girths are popular because they are cheap and easy to maintain, and can be washed. They also permit the air to get to the skin, but they do not last under hard wear.

Nylon Girths shrink badly if they get wet, and if not loosened get over-tight and cause galls. They also stretch.

Leather Girths are good in riding schools, but for trekking they tend to get board-hard and coated with grease and sweat through lack of attention.

Web Girths which are, if used at all, always in pairs and overlap each other so as not to pinch the skin, are not good for trekking and riding holidays. They require constant washing and drying if they are not to collect grease, mud

Fig. 45. Pony sinking down, ears back, tail swishing and hind leg raised when saddle is about to be placed on it, because back is sore

and sweat, get bone hard and rub the animal. They also wear and fray. A single one is dangerous.

Responsibility of the Rider. Should a horse or pony sink down as the saddle is placed upon its back, or "shiver" its skin when touched, it is because its back is tender and painful. If you ride it then the condition will deteriorate. Anyone who has suffered from a blistered heel will sympathize!

If you find a number of lumps or raised surfaces, or even actual raw, bleeding patches, you can be sure that the animal is *not* in good condition. It stands to reason that if the back muscles are fully developed they form a cushion for the saddle, whereas if an animal is lean, and every bone shows, the saddle will rest on the bones of the spine and cause raw places.

Novices may think that there is need to act only when a back is actually raw or the gall caused by the girth actually shows red flesh. This is quite wrong. Lumps or swellings which may develop into abscesses and blisters cause just as much pain, and the animal should be rested at once *before—not after*—the skin breaks or the abscess bursts.

CHAPTER VII

Stable Management and Horse- and Ponymastership

Bedding

PONIES at trekking centres which are out at grass by night, or animals at riding holiday establishments which are likewise, require no bedding as they are only standing in the stable for short periods.

But all stabled animals, be they horse, pony, cow or pig, require a good bed of either straw, peat moss, wood shavings, sawdust, or even dried bracken; but of course straw (wheat or oat—not barley) is best.

Horses and ponies also like something upon which to stale (pass water) as they dislike the splashing on to hard ground or cement. It encourages those which have for any reason failed to do so to place straw or bracken under them.

To give inadequate, or worse still, no bedding, and to allow animals to lie down on bare, damp concrete is not only cruel and inefficient but stupid, as they get sores and contract rheumatism.

Feeding

There is a great art in being what is called a "good feeder".

The basis of it is regularity, feeding individually according to the condition, type or breed, the temperament of the animal, the amount of work it is being asked to do, the length of time out of stable or field each day, and the type of rider.

The food should be well mixed. When feeding a large number of animals, as in trekking centres, a good plan is to place large quantities of the ingredients on a clean cement floor and mix well with a shovel. This makes feeding easier than measuring out each ingredient individually. Each pony or horse should then have a large bucketful twice daily.

All feeds should be slightly damped (not soaked). Once a week all permanently stabled horses and ponies should have a bran mash. This is made either with boiling water poured over a bucket of bran and left to "cook" with a blanket over it, or linseed simmered until it "jellies" and then poured over the bran.

Corn (oats) should be flaky, sweet-smelling and preferably crushed.

Bruised or crushed barley is excellent and can be fed instead of oats or cubes; is nourishing and helps to maintain body heat in winter. Do *not* feed wheat. Flaked maize is fattening and good for maintaining body heat in winter. Bran is almost indispensable as an addition to all feeds and as a laxative; and aids digestion; but may be difficult to obtain. Damp all short feeds very slightly, especially bran.

Quantities to be Fed. It is not possible to give exact quantities because, as has been said before, every horse and pony must be fed with due regard to its size, age, breed or type, condition (some ponies maintain condition where another would starve) and according to the type and amount of work it has to do. Its temperament and the experience of the rider(s) it has to carry have also to be borne in mind, and corn may have to be cut or substituted. But horses and ponies in hard work *must* be fed, whether they are native ponies or thoroughbreds.

No novice can be expected to know how to feed, and in all establishments, therefore, all the food should be given out either by the operator or his staff on the above basis, which is both practical and economical. Many guests thoroughly enjoy feeding their own ponies, which may be encouraged so long as they are given the correct rations.

Short Feeds. All trekking and riding holiday horses and ponies in full work should have "short feeds" and not just hay or grass alone. They should not be asked to work from

10 a.m. to 4–5 p.m. and then have to find their own living, which, on poor pasture, can mean they get no rest at all. In good centres they receive either:

(a) Bruised oats and bran (hay chaff is possible) first thing in the morning, again at mid-day (unless they are grazed when on an all-day trek), and again on return home at night. These should be well mixed and *slightly* damped to fill a large bucket for horses in full work and a smaller bucket for ponies. Total amount of corn per day approx. 9–14 lbs. per horse, 8–9 lbs. per pony, divided into two or three feeds; or

(b) Pony Cubes, with bran if possible but always with plenty of hay or grass and water. They cost no more than other food and will reduce the hay bill, while more water will be drunk.

Correct rations of cubes for trekking ponies in full work: 8–14 lbs. per day in two feeds; (if no grass available at mid-day a few should be carried in a bag attached to the saddle D). Horses proportionately more.

If there is good grazing and animals are out at night, hay need not be fed, but if the grass is short or they are stabled, hay *must* be fed with these cubes to give the necessary bulk feeding—they may eat less hay but drink more water which should be easily available *all the time*.

Other *additional* feeding stuffs are molasses meal which should be added to the short feed (one or two handfuls), sugar beet pulp (always well soaked before feeding), mangolds (after Christmas only), maize (flaked) soaked and fed with other rations to promote heat in body and to fatten, linseed and cod liver oil, and carrots (always sliced).

Other excellent "extras" are "Vi-Minerol", "Codlettes", Boots' "Hi-Vite" and—common salt!

Small ponies ridden by small children *only*, should not be fed on oats as these tend to make them too lively, but they can have pony cubes. Those asked to carry lightweight adults should have their oats like any other pony, related to their work and temperament.

Short feeds should be fed *before* work and at end of day. Time should be given to digest these. Water *before* feeding.

Without "short" feeds horses and ponies are soft and sluggish and will never attain hard condition. Grass-fed animals are soft, easily galled, and "blow" when asked to move at fast paces.

Very Fat Ponies. While ponies that have a tendency to get too fat should be carefully watched, that is no reason for starving them. Some maintain condition when in fact they are hungry and that is why some fat ponies get quite nasty and ill-tempered. So would you!

On the other hand, left on too good grass, for instance in the spring or early summer when the grass is full of proteins, they often contract laminitis, or foot fever, which is extremely painful and in the worst cases, incurable. If they do get it, they should be taken off all grass and oats or heating feeds, and given bran mashes with two tablespoonsful or more, according to size, of Glauber Salts melted down and added to bran. They must have their shoes removed and be brought in from the field and given something soft to stand on, or better still, a clay bed for the affected feet. The disease is so painful that sometimes they cannot stand at all until the attack, which is like gout in humans, passes off. Small native ponies are very liable to this trouble. It can also be caused by concussion and galloping or trotting fast on hard ground.

Feed "Bulk". Hay or grass is essential to horses and ponies and is called "bulk". Without this they cannot properly digest their food.

At some trekking centres, because the ponies have presumably been eating grass all night, no hay is fed in the morning. At others they are given hay, as by midsummer there is unlikely to be much grass, or much "goodness" in what grass there is. The best centres feed corn and bran or cubes *and* hay.

Stabled animals should therefore have a small quantity of hay in the morning at least an hour before work in order to digest it. This should be repeated again at midday unless they have to work again in the afternoon, when they should have a "short feed" only. All should have a large net of hay or the equivalent at night. Even trekking ponies who are going to be turned out at night should be offered hay, unless the grazing is exceptional.

Musty hay, mouldy hay or hay burnt brown can cause colic, broken wind or other troubles. It pays to feed good hay. If at all mouldy, and no other available, damp slightly.

Hay-bags save waste. The large size should be used and tied up well off the ground lest animals get their feet entangled.

Grazing. The quality and quantity of the grass is important.

Fig. 46. Hay-bag correctly tied high off ground

Thistles, buttercups, docks and ragwort are signs of poor land and long, coarse grass is useless, as horses and ponies would rather starve than eat it. If animals are out on this sort of land extra rations must be fed (see also page 123). Ragwort is a slow poison though, luckily, equines leave it alone if there is something else to eat. Its danger is obvious.

WORMS AND THE WORM PROBLEM

This is the hardest thing that modern pony owners have to contend with, because of prevailing conditions.

When grazing was plentiful, owners could ring the changes with their pasture and many also had cattle, poultry and sheep to graze at the same time. There is no doubt that mixed grazing is a good, useful method of keeping land clean and in good heart. Pastures that are grazed by horses year after year get worm-infested and "horse sick".

A change of pasture also facilitates applying lime, which helps to some extent to reduce worm infestation and to increase palatability. Infestation is by eggs and, in some species, by larvae. Nowadays, with so many ponies often confined to one small paddock the whole year round, the worm menace is acute.

This particularly applies to Riding, and especially Trekking Centres, where large numbers of horses and ponies are grazed together, frequently in insufficient acreage and on poor land. It applies even more forcibly at Centres where ponies are hired when needed from local farmers, and which are then all put in together, when they infect the land and so each other.

Actually, the minimum amount of grazing per pony should be one acre.

Regular Worming

Pony owners are advised, therefore, to have their animals treated regularly. It is no use doing so once. Egg worms laid by the adults and passed out on to the grass, hatch out constantly throughout most of the year. It is therefore absolutely essential, in order to get results, to dose at regular intervals, on the advice of a veterinary surgeon, and thereafter at, at least, three to six-monthly intervals.

If, after dosing, a horse or pony is again put out on infected ground, it will of course become re-infected.

Resistance can be a Danger to other Ponies

Some ponies, especially mature ones, are able to develop a certain degree of resistance against worms. They may not therefore show any detectable symptoms. They are, however, likely to carry worms, which continue to spread eggs on the pasture and are therefore a menace to other ponies, especially young ones.

The General Sign of Worms—Harmful Effects

The first harmful effects are gradual and may easily pass unnoticed; namely, a dry, non-thriving coat and loss of condition over the loin, and the beginnings of a pot belly.

There may be a small amount of slime or mucus in the dung. The animal may seem to tire more easily and to blow more than it should after a gallop. Slowly condition and bloom are lost. The coat stares, looks harsh, dull and scurfy despite grooming. The supple, elastic feeling of the skin changes to a tight, "hide-bound" state. The hairs of the tail may become broken and ragged through rubbing. After some weeks a "poverty line" may develop down each buttock and thigh, the animal becomes more pot-bellied, the ribs begin to show and the muscles on either side of the spine under the saddle waste, so that the backbone begins to look rigid and prominent. By this time, the animal may seem to be lazy and slow. It tires readily, blows and sweats and may even begin to stumble.

At any time during this phase of progressive debility the animal may suddenly become severely ill or it may simply continue a gradual decline. It may have a bad attack of colic, develop a temperature, refuse food and show signs of great distress. These symptoms are due to the migration of large numbers of tiny, immature, larval worms from the digestive organs into some important organ of the body— liver, lungs, arteries, or even the heart. The actual symptoms depend on which of these is the most severely damaged.

At this stage, very often the pony can only be saved with difficulty. So much damage has already been done that death is certain, especially in severe cases of redworm, when the larvae invade the anterior mesenteric artery (i.e., the large artery supplying the bowel).

For this reason, most especially in young ponies, worms should never be considered lightly; they are always liable to become dangerous if neglected. The time to get something done to control the worms is *before* any serious symptoms develop. In fact, it is a good policy to treat horses and ponies which have confined or restricted grazing two or three times each year, even though they may not have any worms present or show any symptoms.

Examination of Droppings

It is very advisable to have every horse and pony's droppings subjected to a worm egg "count", especially if they are going to be turned out to grass with others, so that, if an apparently healthy one should be heavily infested, it will be discovered. Sometimes an older horse or pony in very good condition, even fat, may show a high worm "count", for the reason that it has acquired tolerance or resistance which enables it to thrive. Its worms are, however, a danger to other horses and ponies, as it is consistently passing large numbers of eggs on to the grass, which hatch out into larvae to be eaten with the grass by other animals, which may suffer seriously in consequence. This is especially dangerous where foals and yearlings graze the same pasture as old horses.

Droppings should be sent to your veterinary surgeon to be tested, when he will give the "count".

Types of Worms and Internal Parasites

There are several kinds of internal parasites, the principal ones being:

(a) *Bots*. The larvae, or grubs, of a non-biting fly.

(b) *Ascarids*. White, strong, easily seen worms up to a foot in length.

(c) *Strongyles*. Of which there are many types, the chief difference being in size and microscopic structure. Small strongyles include about thirty types—some white, some grey, some red. They are usually less than half an inch in length, and many are very small and not easily seen, and may even be missed by an expert's eye.

Large Strongyles. These are usually $\frac{3}{4}''$ to $\frac{1}{4}''$ long, and are serious. There are three main kinds, of which:—

Strongylus Vulgaris. Is the most dangerous. This is the so-called "red worm", because it sucks blood and has a reddish colour when it has just fed. It may, however, be whitish-grey in colour if it has not recently fed. The larvae of large strongyle worms migrate through the tissues and cause much serious damage.

(d) *Whip or Seat Worms.* About ¾″ long and very thin and wiry.

Treatment for Various Types of Worms

Bots. The maggot stage or larvae of a fly. They are always harmful, especially when present in great numbers. The bot fly lays its tiny, orange-coloured eggs on hairs of the knees and hocks, cannons and flanks of the pony when out at grass from June to October, and especially in August. These hatch out into small maggots which irritate and which the pony, by licking itself, transfers to its stomach, where they grow and develop into full-sized bots. When present in large numbers they cause loss of condition or a staring coat. A pony that appears *not* to thrive, although eating up well, should be suspected of having bots. From about March until late May the bots, about ¾″ long and being mature, come away in the droppings.

If large quantities of the tiny yellow eggs are seen on the pony's legs, etc., these should be regularly removed throughout the summer with an old razor blade or with a singeing lamp, or temporary protection is obtainable by sponging over with one part paraffin to ten parts milk, well shaken up.

There is a new drug incorporated with a bernifuge called Equigard. As this is very lethal to birds in its crystalline form or when passed through the pony in the droppings, animals must be stabled for 48 hours and *droppings not spread on the land or on manure heaps*. Equigard is palatable to ponies and may be administered in the food.

Ascarids. These are common in young horses and ponies up to 3 years old; they are at their highest level in foals and this decreases up to 2 years old. They are uncommon in 4-year-olds and upwards. They can be as thick as a pencil and up to a foot in length.

When present in large numbers, they can cause death from stoppage, rupture of the bowel wall, colic, or the development of a pot belly, or coughing in foals. Loss of condition is a very common result.

PLATE 12. Sun and shade—children having the time of their lives on a riding holiday in Devon.

PLATE 13. A group of trekkers on well-fed, well-cared for ponies, in the charge of a competent Trek Leader.

PLATE 14. A siesta at mid-day. While the riders eat their sandwiches the ponies graze in front of a magnificent *Lake District* backcloth.

It is most important that foals should be dosed for ascarids soon after weaning and again two months later, for it is at these times when they cause most damage and retard growth.

The safest and most effective drug to administer for ascarids is Piperazine (marketed as either Coopane, Pipricide, or Ascarine). At the same time, it will help to control the smaller strongyles and whip worms. It is essential to get a veterinary surgeon to prescribe the correct dose.

Strongyles (including Red Worm). Almost every horse and pony harbours at least some strongyles in its large intestine. Generally, the small strongyles are the more numerous and, when only a few are present, they do little harm.

Large strongyles, however, are always serious and even a few present in a horse or pony for one year may, by laying eggs and infesting the pastures, result in very large numbers being present the following year. Both types are always more serious in foals, yearlings and 2-year-olds than in older animals, though these are by no means immune from them, especially if allowed to get in low condition.

Strongyles are rarely visible to the naked eye in a mass of droppings, but may easily be seen with a lens or if a careful search is made.

Some of the strongyles live by sucking the pony's blood. Others steal the pony's food so that some of the oats, bran or hay eaten by the animal is wasted, since it goes to feed the worms. Some larval form spend their life either wandering through the pony's tissues (such as bowel wall, liver, lungs, kidneys, etc.), or in resting and growing bigger in the bowel wall itself.

In all these situations they cause some pain, aches and damage to the animal, and when present in large numbers make the animal very ill indeed. Ultimate death will occur if they invade the anterior mesenteric artery of the bowel or the small blood vessels of the heart. When they are in the bowel they can be dealt with by drugs, but once they invade the tissues no drug, whether given by mouth or directly into the stomach, can reach them. The general direction of larvae is towards the heart via the blood vessels.

There are several drugs. One of the best is Thiabendazole (marketed under the name of Equizole). It has proved the most satisfactory method so far of dealing with strongyles. It is practically non-toxic and has been found to remove some of the immature stages of worms as well as the mature. There is also some evidence to show that the eggs passed after dosing may be unable to develop into larvae, which is a great advantage as they then do not infect pastures. Piperazine is also used for this purpose but Equizole is even more effective.

There are also some newer drugs, under trade names such as Strongid, Equivurm and Telmin (the latter in syringes for oral dosage). All are safe to use and efficacious and each animal may have his/her preference. It is often a good idea to vary these drugs (*never* mix them or give them at too close an interval) as each drug varies slightly in the expulsion of the various species of strongyle. *But remember that animals dosed with Equigard should be stabled (see under Bots, page* 96).

Whip Worms. These measure about $\frac{3}{4}''$ and their tails are long, thin and pointed, rather like a whip. They occur in the pony's rectum where they produce irritation and cause him to rub his tail. A yellowish-white, sticky discharge can often be seen under the tail.

A veterinary surgeon should be asked to give the pony an enema or to undertake one or other of the various forms of treatment.

Control of Worms

Infestation is scaled by number of eggs per gramme of faeces. For strongyles, 400 e.p.g. is a Pathology, i.e., the worm load is affecting the horse's or pony's condition. (One gramme of faeces is the same size as two thumb nails.)

When to Dose Against Worms

Generally speaking, there are two important periods of the year when it is desirable to dose horses and ponies. The first is in early autumn (September or October), to get rid of the worms which have matured as a result of summer grazing and before the cold, wet weather sets in, with consequent less good quality grass and little or no sunshine. The animal will need all its energies to come through the winter successfully without having to house and feed a large number of parasites as well.

The second, and possibly most important period, is in late winter (February or March). It has been found that worms are less active during winter and lay fewer eggs than during early spring and summer. If they can be got rid of by dosing the pony before the rapid spring egg-laying period begins, so much the better for both pony and pasture.

Where the numbers of worm eggs are very high in ponies, it is necessary to dose three times a year, the extra dose being given in May or June. Actually, dosing every six weeks is recommended by the makers of Equizole, but, unless badly infected, every two months should be enough. This frequency, however, is usually only necessary when there has been much previous neglect, when pastures are badly infested and very "horse sick", or when the ponies are not putting on condition.

It must not be thought, however, that these are the only times to dose. When a new pony is bought, no matter at what time of year, it is a good plan to dose it at once before putting it out to pasture with others. It is a very good idea to keep any newcomer stabled until it has been tested or dewormed, when it should be kept stabled for two or three days before letting it out to grass, either alone or with others.

Also, if at any time between the regular dosing periods an animal shows symptoms of having worms, it should be treated at once.

Young Ponies, including Foals

These should be dosed for strongyle at approximately 4 months and thereafter every eight weeks, with whatever drug your veterinary surgeon advises. Or go to your local veterinary surgery and ask for a worm dose, stating age and size of the foal. Foals will not eat pellets and require the dose in powder form, and pellets bought from a chemist are therefore useless.

Precautions to be taken when Dosing

Although modern drugs are far safer than many of the older ones, it should be appreciated that worm medicines can be harmful and that care should be taken to give the correct dose according to the age and size of horse or pony. If the dose is not properly measured, it may either be too small to kill the worms or too large for the size or age of the animal, which may then become slightly ill. The correct amount must be given.

A veterinary surgeon should look at the horse or pony and advise on the kind of drug and the amount that should be given.

Worm medicines are available from chemists who stock veterinary products. They are made by reliable drug manufacturing firms and most have instructions on the labels. Undoubtedly the best and the safest of these is Equizole, which can be bought in pellet form in containers which have instructions clearly marked on them. It is expensive, but is popular not only because it is effective but because it cuts out the necessity of calling in a veterinary surgeon. This is a danger, however. It is very much better to obtain the advice of a veterinary surgeon and to diagnose the type of worm before embarking on treatment.

Preparation for Worming

Purging and starvation before dosing used to be recommended in the past. Mercifully, this is not necessary with up-to-date remedies. A small bran mash the night before dosing is useful when dealing with stabled animals, and only a little hay should be given that night. This is not necessary with animals out at grass.

For stabled animals, and those worked off grass, it is important that no violent exercise should be allowed during the first 48 hours after dosing, though a little walking exercise may be given on the second day. Thereafter, exercise can be resumed as usual.

You will find that Equizole, in powder or pellet form, is eaten readily by most horses and ponies. A few will pick out the pellets from a feed and leave them, when it will be necessary to mix the powder form in a little damp bran and crushed oats. Very fussy feeders will have to be tempted with molasses, sugar or what have you. It is possible to obtain a "dosing gun" for administering worm doses in a liquid form, but unless you are familiar with its use, it would be better to get your veterinary surgeon to show you how to handle the pony whilst dosing. Telmin is dispensed in a syringe for oral dosage.

A worm dose may also be given by stomach tube, but only by a veterinary surgeon.

When dosing with the Piperazine compounds, the animal may be given its normal feed in, say, half an hour or so. Dosing with Equizole, the powder or pellets can simply be put in the normal feed or, if in the summer when out at grass, in a feed of bran and oats.

After Care

If the horse or pony is in poor condition, good feeding should follow until it has picked up into proper condition.

This period of good feeding following dosing is very important where there has been much loss of condition.

Method of Dosing

(1) *The Piperazine Compounds (i.e., Coopane, Pipricide, Ascarine, etc.)*

These compounds will remove ascarids and whip worms as well as the smaller strongyles. They also have some effect in destroying a proportion of the more serious larger strongyles.

They can be given in safety even to young animals, are easily given, and usually readily eaten in a mash.

Each of the Piperazine Compound preparations has instructions for dosage on the label or on a separate sheet. These should be strictly followed and, since they vary, it is impossible to give more precise details here. But, as before stated, it is much safer to obtain a veterinary surgeon's advice rather than risk the life of the animal by a mistake or possible over-dosage.

If treatment fails and the animal does not begin to improve in condition within two or three weeks' time after dosing, something other than worms may be responsible and further expert advice should be obtained without loss of time.

(2) *Equizole*

The horse and pony formula is marketed by Merck, Sharp and Dohme, Ltd., and is made up either as a pinkish powder or in pellet form.

Apart from its efficiency, its advantages are that it is practically tasteless and therefore, in nine times out of ten, readily acceptable, and that no previous starvation is necessary. It is dispensed in tins containing 30 grammes in powder form, which is the recommended dose for a pony weighing 500 lbs., or in pellet form, when the dosage is clearly marked on the label.

Although it is practically non-toxic, it is essential as with all worm remedies, to administer the correct dose to obtain results, and we repeat that it is wisest and saves time to ascertain through a veterinary surgeon what type of worms your animal has before you start dosing.

Equizole has been shown to be effective against both large and small strongyles (including red worm) and also ascarids (at a higher dosage level). It has no effect on stomach bots.

Indications are that in addition to suppression of egg production and expulsion of adult worms, Equizole kills worms at other stages of their development, with obvious advantages such as keeping fields and paddocks free of infestation.

After Treatment

Again it is emphasised that the horse's or pony's condition should be built up after treatment with good feeding and not a lot of work, until it is in good condition again. This particularly applies to those that have suffered from red worm, as these cause anaemia and consequent listlessness.

Vitamin B12, administered by a veterinary surgeon, can be used to increase the red cell count, which is often decreased by heavy infestation of strongyles.

WARNING

Illness, even death, can result from rule of thumb advice which, while perhaps applicable in the majority of cases, may need modifying for individuals.

Furthermore, treatment to-day depends so much upon the identification of the worms which are causing the trouble that it is not something which can always be left safely to the animal's owner. This is the danger in being able to procure veterinary products direct from the chemist or drug store, so saving veterinary fees. On the other hand, if an owner cannot afford these fees say, twice a year, then surely he has no right to be keeping a horse or pony.

Donkeys

Donkeys, which are often turned out with horses and ponies, suffer occasionally from lung worm, which causes a chronic cough, sometimes even bronchitis and pneumonia. This is a condition which your veterinary surgeon will deal with.

Unfortunately there is no worm dose which is 100% effective at the present time. Tetramosole can be used, which will reduce the numbers, or a very large dose of Thiabendazole (ten times the normal dose and therefore very expensive) is the best available at present.

Why Waste Food, and therefore money, feeding worms?
In short—Why "Waste" Your Pony?

Grass Sickness

Work is still going on in investigating the cause of this, but at present it is true to say that, while a lot is known concerning the things which do *not* cause it, there is still little firm or definite information, apart from profound nerve degeneration which occurs, which indicates the real cause.

A veterinary surgeon should be called in at once should symptoms appear which are suspicious. They may take two or three days to develop, but should the animal stagger in its walk, shiver, become more or less unconscious, or be averse to lying down but lean for support on any convenient object, breathe in a peculiar manner, or have spasms like those in tetanus—these are all signs of possible grass sickness. It can, however, be confused with severe colic. Whichever it is, a veterinary surgeon should be called in.

If grass sickness is confirmed, the kindest thing to do is to put the animal down humanely at home, and done by a v.s. Even if the animal recovers, which is rare, they are never again up to much work.

Shoeing in Trekking and Riding Holiday Establishments

When Working. No horse or pony should be worked without shoes. Hooves should not be allowed to grow too long, thereby placing a strain on the back tendons of the legs. Old shoes wear thin and are easily displaced and because thin and sharp cause cuts and wounds to legs.

The clenches (or nails) with which the shoes are attached to the hooves should not be allowed to grow out as they then knock against the opposite leg and cause wounds. Clenches *can* be knocked down temporarily with a hammer should they become prominent but this can cause more harm than good and the animal should be re-shod as soon as possible.

Loose shoes make a clicking noise which is easily heard, and should be reported to the operator or his staff. The shoes should be nailed on again as soon as possible or removed altogether. It is dangerous to leave them hanging.

Shoes which for any reason get out of place may then bear on the seat of corns and cause lameness.

Cracks and splits running up the hooves are not a good thing, and should have the attention of the farrier or they will almost certainly cause lameness. Hooves should be well oiled especially round the top where the hair grows. All working animals should be looked over daily for foot troubles.

Not Working. Animals not working and out at grass should

have their shoes removed. *All shoes should be taken off at the end of the trekking season* if the ponies are to be out at grass and their hooves pared throughout the winter according to

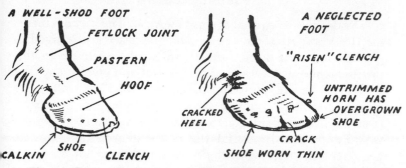

Fig. 47. Correct shoeing

Fig. 48. Split and cracked hooves through shoes being left on

Fig. 49. Knocking and brushing causing wounds

growth and to prevent them from splitting and cracking and causing corns. (Fig. 48).

There is an axiom in the horse world: "No Foot—No

Horse". A stitch in time saves nine so far as horses' feet are concerned.

Grooming Ponies

Trekking Centres and out at Grass by Night. The arrangements for this vary. At some centres the guests are encouraged to groom their own ponies and there can be no harm in this practice, indeed it adds to their interest and gives them confidence in their mounts. At others, those who are willing are allowed to "help" but are shown how by experienced staff (this applies particularly to riding holiday stables), which would appear to be by far the best system as no complete beginner can know what to do without being shown.

But if you are expected or encouraged to groom a pony and clean its equipment, do it properly.

Novices should on no account be left to handle the ponies without at least some instruction and help. Some guests pick it up very quickly and by the end of the week have grasped the essentials; others find it more difficult.

When to Groom—Trekking Centres. The best time to groom is early in the morning before the animals go out riding or trekking.

Having been brought in from the field and given their breakfast while the guests have theirs, all should be given a good brushing all over with a dandy brush, especially where the sweat crystals from the previous day's trek have formed and the scurf been raised, i.e. under the saddle, girths or any other straps. Sweat crystals are sharp and quickly cause sore backs if left on. Dry mud should be removed, either with the dandy brush or with the help of a rubber curry comb (an old piece of motor tyre does as well) but wet mud should be left until dry and then removed as above.

Horses' and ponies' legs should *not* be washed, as if the water gets into the hollow of the heel, the skin chaps and cracks and causes severe lameness. For the same reason the tuft of hair at their heels should not be cut off. This is Nature's protection from wet and damp and prevents sore, cracked heels by inducing the rain and wet to run down the hair and to drip on the ground instead of into the hollow of the heel.

On returning home, the pony should, if not hot and sweaty, again be brushed over and the scurf removed. The fitter the animal is, the less it sweats.

If hot and sweating, by far the best thing is to turn it straight out in the field where it can have a roll and move about, will quickly dry off and seldom, if ever, catch cold. It can either be fed in the field, or better still, brought in and fed in the stable when cooled off.

If it is not possible to turn it out in the field, then its ears and back should be rubbed dry, or the saddle left on with the girth loosened until it dries. It is very important to dry and get warm a horse's or pony's ears. Cold, sweaty ears are an indication that the animal is chilled.

When the saddle is left on, care should be taken to tie the pony up with its head high so that it cannot get down and roll on the saddle. To remove a saddle from a hot and sweating animal immediately it returns from work, frequently causes a sore back.

Grooming in Riding Holiday Stables where Animals are Stabled Day and Night. If any animal returns to the stable still hot and sweating, a good plan is to place some straw along the top of its back and throw a rug over the whole until the sweat dries.

"Strapping" is much more elaborate and in the best stables a skilled job. No novice can be expected to know the routine or how to carry it out, but any guest on holiday who is keen to learn should be given every possible help and encouragement as part of their holiday schedule.

Grooming Equipment in Trekking Centres

This should, of course, be supplied and should include these essentials:

Dandy Brushes for removing scurf, sweat marks and mud (when dry).

Metal Curry Comb for cleaning scurf, etc., from dandy and other brushes, but never on the animals themselves nor for manes and tails, which should be carefully brushed out with a dandy brush.

Rubber Curry Comb or piece of old motor tyre, excellent for removing old hair or obstinate patches of dried mud.

Oil for applying to the hooves of the animals, especially at the top where the hair grows to promote growth of new horn and so prevent cracking and splitting (as in finger nails).

Brush to apply Oil.

Stable cloths or "rubbers" for drying sweaty back and flanks (wisps made of hay are even better).

Water buckets, brooms, pitchforks, shovels, stable barrow and "skips" for removing dung, etc.

A warm rug or two in case of illness.

Grooming Equipment in Riding Holiday Centres

All of the above but more—such as body and water brushes and a clipping machine, rugs, day and night rollers for all clipped-out animals. Also farrier's tools such as buffer, hammer, paring knife, etc., for use in emergencies. Bandages (wool).

Care of Equipment in Trekking Centres

"Tack-cleaning" is not required to be done by guests at some centres whereas at others it is. Most guests enjoy learning to do this while the experienced like helping.

In trekking centres where little or no fast work is done, and because of the large numbers being dealt with, operators use such preparations as Koa-chalin or Flexalan, which is easily applied. Even if it is not possible in the time available to wash and dry the "tack" (as all equipment is called) provided it is soft and supple and therefore safe, this is adequate.

Required: Warm water, sponges and rags for washing off grease and mud, chamois leather for drying. Tins of Koa-chalin, or Flexalan, saddle soap, and rags and polishers for applying these. Duraglit and chamois leathers for cleaning bits, and stirrup irons. Neat's foot oil to apply to any leather which is stored or put by for the winter.

Care of Equipment in Riding Holiday Centres

A much higher standard is to be expected at these than at purely trekking centres.

All leather should be washed, if not daily, then twice or three times a week, with warm water to remove grease and mud, and dried with a chamois leather. Good saddle soap should then be applied vigorously. In first-class stables, the "tack" is, of course, cleaned daily.

Again, leather not in use or to be stored away, should have Neats' foot oil applied before storing to keep it from getting hard and brittle, or it may not be usable by the following season.

Stirrup Irons and Bits. These should be kept clean by washing and bright by polishing; although this is important, this is not so important as the care of leather to which they are attached.

Bits can easily be rinsed in water to remove froth or chewed grass, etc., *immediately they are removed.*

Saddle or "Tack" Room. Every trekking or riding holiday establishment should have a properly organized room or shed in which to keep its equipment, known as the "tack" room. It is wise to keep a stove in this room to prevent mildew getting into the leather and rotting it.

Each saddle should have its own bracket or saddle horse and a bracket or hook underneath for the bridle or headstall (and in trekking stables either a halter rope or rope halter) with the name of the pony above or below it. This avoids muddle and saves valuable time, and helps to ensure that each animal gets its right equipment which fits it.

"Dressing" Saddles. When removed from the animals' backs, saddles should have the girths folded and tucked under the right-hand saddle flap or they should be laid across the seat of the saddle (see page 50).

The stirrup irons should be pulled up to the top of the back strap of the leathers, and the loop of the leathers passed through the iron, where they remain until wanted again (see Fig. 50). Dangling irons cause accidents and all stirrup irons should be put up in this way when the rider

Fig. 50. Saddles and bridles on brackets in tack room with name of pony above

dismounts for any reason and also before attempting to re-place the saddle on the animal's back.

Laying down a Saddle. Saddles should not be thrown care-lessly on the ground. The arches inside the leather break easily, the leather scratches, etc. They should therefore be placed upright on the front arch so that the linings can air and no harm comes to the saddles (see page 47).

CHAPTER VIII

Post Trekking

POST trekking, that is, riding a distance, camping out overnight and riding on the next day, and so on for varying
periods from two days to a week or longer, should not be
undertaken lightly or by inexperienced or novice riders. It
entails a certain amount of technical knowledge to be suc-
cessful from the point of view of both the rider and his mount.

If a long trek is contemplated of three days and upwards,
quite extensive arrangements have to be made ahead to
make certain that the route to be ridden is open and pass-
able, and that food and shelter is available at the end of
each day for horse and rider.

A series of fields where the ponies can run loose at night is
important. These should be completely separate from the
field in which the riders' tent may be pitched, so that the
two do not get mixed up together.

A week or so spent pony trekking can be a very enjoyable
holiday. Unfortunately it is not always so. Ponies are expensive to keep properly; partly because of this, and partly
sometimes through ignorance of the right way of treating
ponies, they are underfed, and too small and weak to carry
heavy adults. The holiday-makers are given little or no instruction, and as a result they can add unknowingly to the
maltreatment of the ponies. The equipment used is often
unsuitable and causes pain and discomfort to both rider and
pony.

Some of the most enjoyable trekking in this country is
amongst the wild country of mountain and moorland.
Crossing this sort of country on ponyback is not as easy as
it looks, and needs special training, if both are to gain enjoyment from it. Make sure, therefore, that the first holiday

you spend like this is at a place where you will get sufficient instruction. There can be few pleasures to equal riding a clever and courageous pony over beautiful country, crossing the tops of high hills, enjoying, with the pony, a feeling of pride and satisfaction.

To achieve this, both pony and rider must work hard together, climbing up and down steep slopes, picking a way through bogs, crossing rough, stony ground, and fording rushing streams, occasionally having to dismount and leap over the most difficult going.

It is fair to do this only if the rider and pony are fit to do it. The rewards are many because the difficulties are great. Strenuous effort on the part of the pony and the rider are needed. Obedience and trust are required from the pony; self-discipline, unselfishness and understanding from the rider.

In trekking across mountainous country it is not advisable for anyone—however experienced—to go alone; an accident can so easily happen when there is no one to go for help, and quite a minor mishap may have fatal consequences as a result. If this advice is disregarded, a person going alone should leave with a responsible person full details of route and expected time of arrival.

Those without experience of riding across mountains must ride together with an experienced leader, and it really is essential to get thorough instruction and training in the special technique of riding in mountainous and difficult country—not only from the point of view of safety but also for the safety and welfare of the animals concerned.

The "tack" (and especially the saddles) has to have special attention to prevent sores and if the trek is for more than two or three days a pack-horse or pony has to be taken or provisions sent ahead of schedule. If a pack animal is to be taken it needs a skilled person to decide on the saddle and equipment (what to take and what not to take)—and above all, how to pack it.

With careful organization, food for ponies and riders can be sent on ahead to post offices *en route*, addressed to the rider, "poste restante". It would be possible to send on a parcel of 15 lb.—which is the maximum which can be sent—one and a half day's supply of Pony Cubes. Another small parcel could contain food for the rider. It is also possible by this system to have fresh clothing awaiting you, while soiled clothing can be returned in the same wrapper from the post office.

A tremendous amount of goodwill will usually be found everywhere when journeying on horseback. People appear to like to see parties travelling independently across country. It seems to get hold of their imagination, but it cannot be over-emphasized that this should not be undertaken without pre-knowledge and instruction and on suitable, fit animals with the proper equipment. In Wales, especially, not much post trekking is undertaken in view of the difficulty of the terrain and the great number of streams and lakes, which, however, provide natural water resources for both horse and rider.

The following suggestions are for post treks of short duration only. Instructions are of the simplest but should be adequate if followed carefully.

Horses and Ponies Suitable for Post Trekking

Horses and ponies used for post trekking should above all be sound with good limbs and feet, or you may find yourself walking home. They should be up to weight and be good "do-ers", i.e. they should not become upset by moving away from home, and therefore eat their food up at night. It is essential that they should be corn-fed previously and that they be made fit by regular daily exercise of increasing distances for some weeks before embarking—this, of course, according to the distances to be ridden. They should be well and carefully shod all round before leaving home. For really long distances Arabs are hard to beat as they have the necessary courage, but they need more care than the commoner bred types. Native ponies, especially pedigree ones, are ideal. (See under "Large Type Breeds of Native Ponies", pages 60–70.) Thoroughbreds are NOT suitable.

They should not be smaller than 13.2 h.h. (unless children

are taking part) and preferably from 14.1 to 15 h.h. with plenty of bone and substance. They should be in fit and hard condition before embarking. It is advisable to use larger animals, not only from humane motives but because there will otherwise be no space on their backs for the necessary equipment plus the rider. It would mean, for example, that the saddle bag would rest on the loins and kidneys, and would be similar to a "hiker" carrying his rucksack on his "buttocks".

The following equipment will be needed by two persons on a post trek of two days, i.e. one night, or at most two, away from Headquarters.

Equipment Required

1 tent made of light Egyptian cotton weighing not more than 8½ lb. complete with tent poles and pegs contained in its own valise, unless it is intended to sleep in barns.

2 Army Officer-type iron arch saddles with plenty of brass "Ds" in front and behind to which to attach equipment.

2 down-filled sleeping-bags.

2 light macintosh ground-sheets.

2 pairs of leather Army wallets, procurable from Adams, Saddlers, Carnaby Street, London, W.1.

1 Bleuet Butane gas Primus stove.

1 light aluminium billy-can (per two persons).

2 plastic mugs.

2 tin plates.

2 knives, forks and spoons.

Tins of feed, etc. (see separate suggested list).

Two light canvas bags in which to put 10 lb. 7 oz. *per Pony* of Horse and Pony Cubes, to be given in two feeds each—on the first evening and the second morning. It is presumed that the ponies are fed on the morning of leaving and on return at the end of the second day.

Where water has to be obtained from taps, a canvas bucket will be required.

Packing of Equipment

Note : This refers to one pony only.

Each 10 lb. 7 oz. of Horse Cubes should be divided into two equal portions and placed in two small canvas bags. The first of these should then be placed at the bottom of the oblong saddlebag. The sleeping-bag should be folded into a sausage roll 3 ft. long; inside it place all personal clothing and the ground-sheet. Place this roll inside the oblong saddlebag and into it pack billy-can and other hardware utensils, taking care that all hard surfaces are kept well away from the pony's back and that there is a flat surface in the middle of the saddlebag which should have a strap placed firmly round it exactly in the centre. Before closing the open end of the saddlebag, place the second canvas bag containing the other half of the Horse Cubes at the top end, thus retaining an equal balance of weight on either side of the pony. Gather the open ends of the saddlebag into a "neck", twist the lacing, wrap firmly round the neck and tie tightly so that the small articles cannot fall out.

The saddlebag is then placed across the back of the saddle; it should be as flat and soft as possible across the spine and of equal weight either side, or it will slew round. It is again emphasized that no hard objects should be allowed any-where near the pony's spine or skin. The end of the strap which is round the saddlebag is then passed through the "D" in the centre of the cantle (or back of the saddle) and secured. If the weight has been properly distributed and the saddlebag securely packed it will remain exactly in the middle, but to ensure this two more straps must be attached round each end of the saddlebag and through the side "Ds" of the saddle. *These straps should be tightened gradually, first at one side a little, then the other side a little and so on to get equal weight and pressure.* The saddlebag should gradually be rolled towards the back of the rider and the straps pulled as tight as possible in order to lift the weight off the animal's loins and kidneys as much as possible. Straps with buckles and tongues will be found easier than slide buckles. All strap ends should be tucked away and not left hanging loose.

In the leather Army wallets should be placed the Thermos flask, sandwich case, first aid kit, buffer and hammer (in case of trouble with the animal's feet), a camera, if wanted, and any other small articles. These wallets should then be thrown over the *front* arch of the saddle so that they hang down on either side of the saddle flap in front of the rider's knees. The centre strap is attached to the small "D" in the front arch of the saddle and further straps are passed round the centre of each wallet and through the "D" at the front of

Fig. 51. Packing an Army saddle for post trekking

each saddle flap to prevent flapping. The total weight of the saddlebag at the back of the saddle should be between 30 and 35 lb. and of the wallets when full 6 lb. The heaviest item is, of course, the pony's rations.

If a tent is taken it should be placed in its valise on top of the oblong saddlebag behind the rider and tied securely. The rider's macintosh goes across the front arch over the wallets, rolled up as flat and as tightly as possible and tied securely to the saddle "Ds".

Clothing

Clothing depends on the time of the year, but should be as

practical as possible. The absolute minimum of spare clothing for the rider should consist of a pair of slacks, clean shirt
for sleeping in, a spare sweater, washing kit and towel, and
a light hat of some sort for wear in hot sun or rain. In
addition a hard hat is a must at all centres.

Riding kit: Jodphurs are the correct and most comfortable
riding kit, but twill trousers can be worn especially on wet
days and if macintoshes are too expensive. Many young
people appear quite happy in jeans, especially for trekking
when the pace is mainly at the walk with an occasional
slow trot. Cotton shirts, light or thick woollen ones for cold
days can replace hacking jackets. Cavalry twill slacks, an
Aertex shirt or anorak (or parka) are both suitable and
comfortable.

Footwear: Shoes are the hardest thing to advise on. If
the weather is very wet, gum-boots are the answer, but
they are hot in the summer. A light pair of spare walking
shoes can be taken along, but *never* wear riding boots as
they are uncomfortable to walk in, especially down un-
rideable slopes, and comfortable footwear is essential.
Never ride in plimsolls as these permit the foot to slip
through the iron, where the foot may get fixed in the event
of a fall. If plimsolls are taken, they should only be used
for wear in camp. Always wear shoes or boots *with* heels.

Rations

The following is a suggested list of rations, for one rider per
day:

2 oz. of butter or margarine.
1½ oz. of cheese.
2 packets biscuits.
2½ oz. jam or marmalade.
2½ oz. sugar (lump).
2 oz. chocolate.
3 oz. Kendal mint cake (a famous nourishing provider for
   anyone taking hard exercise).
2 oz. raisins/dates.
½ oz. tea, cocoa or Nescafé.

3 oz. condensed milk.

2 oz. Quaker oats.

½ oz. soup powder.

1½ oz. Pom.

2–2½ oz. tinned meat.

2 oz. bacon.

Salt, Oxo, Marmite, matches, toilet paper.

Here is a suggested menu based on the above rations, to include two main cooked meals and one very light lunch:

Breakfast. Porridge, fried bacon, biscuits, butter and marmalade, coffee or tea. Eggs can be obtained *en route*.

Lunch. Carried in the pocket—biscuits, cheese, chocolate, raisins or dates.

Supper. Meat stew, mashed potatoes, biscuits, cheese and coffee.

Pitching a Tent

Choose a level, sheltered site on smooth ground with water near by. The tent should be pitched with the entrance away from the prevailing wind and weather. Care should be taken not to touch the fabric if it is raining as this will make it leak. The strain on the guy ropes should be equal and as much shelter as possible sought, such as the lee of a wall.

When living in a tent the minimum amount of movement is advisable if raining, as touching the fabric causes leaking.

Riders should sleep head to tail. Wet clothes should be kept well away from other clothes as they can make them damp also. The sleeping-bag should be unrolled only when needed, and cooking should be undertaken in the shelter of the entrance.

All equipment, Primus stove, sleeping-bags, etc., should be well tested before leaving.

Hygiene

Latrines should be sited well away from the camp and covered over with spoil, rocks or stones after use.

All tins should be thoroughly burned out, bashed flat and buried. All rubbish should be burnt and no litter left about. Care should be taken not to pollute water.

Varying Paces and Other Hints

It is a good thing to trot for periods when the journey is suitable, as this uses different muscles from those used when walking. This applies to both horse and rider. To vary the pace refreshes both. For the same reason, wise riders dismount and lead their animals for ten minutes or so after $1\frac{1}{2}$ hours riding.

Fig. 52. Pony rolling on saddle, thus breaking the tree, which then causes sores

Horses and ponies may drink at every stream if they wish. They should indeed be encouraged to go into streams and pools, as this cools and freshens their legs. At midday an hour's rest should be taken, when everything should be removed from the animal's back while it is turned loose to graze and rest. Should there be any danger of their straying, which is not likely, they should, of course, be watched. But it is fatal to leave saddles on, as a hot and tired horse or pony invariably gets down and rolls, which almost invariably breaks the saddle tree (which in turn causes saddle sores and is expensive to mend).

Route

It is a good idea to take a one-inch map of the district to be ridden over and a small notebook in which to keep a "log". The route should be carefully mapped out before starting out each day. Help with this can be obtained from the Ancient Order of Pack Riders (Secretary, Mrs. Williams, Four Ways, Blackpool Corner, Axminster, Devon). Any information on routes that you ride successfully and which you enjoy should be sent to her to be recorded for the use of other potential riders.

First Aid for the Pony

It is hoped that there will be no need for first aid but it is wise to take a packet of Acrimide (sulphanilamide) puffer pack and a small tube of Savlon for cuts and scratches (use either or both) with you on trek, and a small bottle of oil of citronella or an aerosol "Extra-tail" against flies.

First Aid for the Rider

Tin of Elastoplast dressings, "Waspeeze" for stings, potash of permanganate for snake bite, Savlon for both rider and pony, and anti-sunburn cream applied before starting.

Pulse

To take the pulse of an equine, lay three fingers inside and along the lower jaw, where the artery may be felt a little in front of the fleshy part of the cheek. Gently press artery with middle finger against surface of bone. Usual rate is 40 beats a minute for well-bred animals, 35 a minute for commoners and ponies. The younger the animal, the quicker the pulse.

Temperature

Average temperature of a healthy horse or pony is about 100° Fahrenheit, varying between 99° to 101°. Temperature may be one degree higher in a very young or very old animal.

Consider your Mount

Always be considerate to the animal you are riding. Dismount and walk down long hills or very steep inclines. This relieves not only your mount but also your own knees. Do not forget to dismount, loosen the girth a hole or two, and walk the last quarter of a mile at the end of a long day to let the blood circulate under the saddle before it is removed.

Be sure to check for any sign of a sore back under the saddle before you mount and when you remove saddle. Also look to see that there are no loose shoes or risen nails (called clenches).

Horses and ponies dislike raucous laughter and harsh voices, but enjoy singing and whistling, especially when they are tired. So sing and whistle if you like, but when you speak, moderate your voice, which should be either calm and firm, or soothing, according to the need of the moment. More can be done by the voice than the whip or even the rein, when managing horses or ponies, provided that the voice is calm and yet conveys authority and confidence. Both horses and ponies sense the rider's mood, and especially his fears. They are quite likely to share it, so self-control is as important as control of the animal. This is another reason why riding is an excellent character builder.

The horse or pony you ride must respect you, but he should also be your companion and not merely a means of conveyance, like a bicycle. Only when you and your mount are one will you get the most out of riding and trekking.

CHAPTER IX

Starting a Trekking and Riding Holiday Centre

MANY centres have been and are still being opened by completely inexperienced persons without adequate capital and facilities, using unsuitable animals and are in charge of unqualified, often totally ignorant, people.

A project started on these lines can only be "money down the drain" and tend to bring the whole trekking and riding holiday movement into disrepute.

Before anyone attempts to start a trekking or riding holiday centre it is essential to know something about the subject. No one would undertake such a responsible job without this very necessary knowledge, unless he or she is merely out for a gamble by exploiting both the public and the animals involved or is prepared to lose money in the long run.

The operator, if he does not himself have the necessary knowledge, should be well advised to pay a really qualified person to run the centre, and not rely, as some do, on inferior labour. No organization or individual should embark on a project unless prepared to spend at least enough money to provide adequate grazing and stabling, suitable animals bought for their economical and utility value, and sound equipment. To buy too small, light-boned or young animals just because they are cheap, cannot be economically sound when it has been proved without doubt that the larger ponies are a better financial proposition for trekking and the stout, tough, cobby type of horse, or cob (with a few exceptions) the best and most economical types for riding holidays.

Poor quality saddles, leather and girths are a dead loss, and it always pays to feed and care for the animals and to shoe them well and regularly.

Some centres, especially in Wales, do not own their ponies. They hire them, and in many cases those provided are quite unsuitable, many being small, narrow, light-boned three-year-olds (even much younger) which should not be working at all. It is amazing how adults can bring themselves to bestride these wretched little ponies, some of them from 11.2 h.h. to 12.2 h.h., upon which they look ridiculous, quite apart from the inhumanity of it. The argument frequently advanced is that these ponies have carried their former owners for centuries. This is true, but the ponies being bred then were the old-fashioned "Moor" type which had a great deal more bone and substance than their modern counterparts; besides—because a thing has been done for centuries does not necessarily make it right. Take cock-fighting, or bull-baiting, for example! There is more excuse for the Egyptian "fellaheen" who works an unfit horse because he has to do so from dire necessity than there is for people in this country, who should know better, to hire out or ride unfit or unsuitable horses and ponies.

To start off with there must be adequate grazing with water always available, preferably running water. Grass is both desirable and advisable, especially when dealing with native ponies, which have proved the best and most economical proposition, particularly for trekking. To be able to turn them out to graze overnight and for the rest periods is of the greatest practical and economical value.

Trekking ponies in riding holiday centres suffer from swollen joints, splints, sore shins, sprained backs, etc., like any other horse or pony, and to have somewhere they can be rested and relaxed is not only wise, but economical. They also do better and are happier turned out during the night in spring and summer, while they can also remain out most of the winter *provided they are fed accordingly* (see Chapter VI).

Grazing

The minimum grazing should be an acre per pony. If it is very good old pasture which has been well "done" care will have to be taken that ponies do not thereby get laminitis, especially in the spring and early summer when the grass is full of proteins. Very coarse, long grass, on the contrary, is sour. Horses and ponies would rather starve than eat it. It is fit only for bullocks and they have to be hungry ones! Likewise, grass growing under trees has no food value, through lack of the sun's rays; nor has that grown on poor, sandy soil.

Another problem is that when a number of ponies are turned out together the ground gets both horse-sick and worm-infested (see Chapter VII).

The ideal is to graze ponies with cattle, sheep and even poultry and to have a change of pasture to enable re-seeding, liming, dressing with basic slag, etc., to be done.

Herbs, Good and Bad

While many herbs are extremely beneficial, docks and buttercups are useless, while some herbs are definitely poisonous, e.g. deadly nightshade, ragwort, yew-tree, hemlock, St. John's Wort, laburnum, and nearly all ornamental shrubs such as laurel, rhododendron, privet bushes. Acorns are an accumulative poison, especially if eaten in large quantities when green.

On the other hand, certain herbs, notably dandelion, chicory, clover, couch-grass, vetches, nettles (if cut down and left to wither, when the sting goes out of them), even knapweed, etc., are valuable. This is proved by the fact that so many gipsies' ponies and horses are fit and well through feeding along the hedgerows, where any number of beneficial herbs grow. It is a mistake to get rid of all herbage, but the useless herbs should certainly be removed or killed by some of the new weed-killers, which destroy them but not the grass, notably thistles.

Water

Water should always be available at all times; running water is best, especially if there is a gravel bottom. If a tank is used a ball-cock should be fitted, and covered over. In frosty weather the ice should be broken daily.

Fencing

Because of the cost of timber, and in order to control cattle and sheep, which are very beneficial to the land, barbed wire is usual nowadays. If this is to be used it should be pulled very taut and not left loose, trailing or near the ground, when the heels of the ponies are liable to get caught up and badly injured; hundreds of animals are damaged by barbed wire every year, some permanently. If it can be afforded, operators are advised to fit a top bar made of timber to a fence, with the barbed wire underneath, and so maybe save pounds by loss or injury of valuable animals. Barbed wire piercing a leg near a joint can end in permanent stiffness in that joint owing to the joint oil running out.

Wintering Out

Horses/ponies, whether from trekking or riding holiday stables, when turned out in wintertime should have all their shoes removed, and their feet should be regularly trimmed throughout the winter. If their coats have been clipped they should be allowed to grow or they should have their rugs removed for a short period before being turned loose, to harden them off.

That they must be fed unless the grass is adequate and good, and always in hard weather, is obvious, yet there are many owners who seem to take a pride in announcing that their animals "can 'live' on the smell of an oil rag". The stamina of our native ponies especially is thus exploited to a disgraceful extent. Every pony needs hay in winter according to the state of the weather and the amount of grass. True, if there is plenty of the latter they will refuse hay, but frequently ponies are seen standing about in wet, muddy fields which are virtually as bare as a carpet or with only long, coarse grass which, as previously remarked, horses and ponies will rather starve than eat out at grass. For larger types 16 lb.

of hay per day is the minimum, less according to size. Thin-skinned horses should be provided with a New Zealand rug fed on short rations, such as oats, maize, cubes, etc., to retain the heat in their bodies, but it is better and more economical to bring them in at night. Foals by thoroughbreds or Arabs should be stabled at night in their first year and fed; even those from pure-bred native stock benefit from this treatment. But native ponies running wild in their native haunts,

Fig. 53. Pony out wintering in wind and rain with no shelter, no food or grass, inadequate water

are far better off than those confined in small, shelterless, worm-infested paddocks, for they at least can find their own windbreaks and have what is called "range", whilst also having more opportunity of finding food. Windbreaks are invaluable for out-wintering animals of all kinds and care should be taken to feed in the lee of these away from the prevailing wind. Taking this little extra trouble will save money.

Also throwing hay down just anywhere, in mud and dung, is sheer waste. Hay-bags or hay-racks save money. These should be placed away from each other to prevent kicking and biting of jealous feeders. Young animals should be watched, as otherwise, if turned out with older ones, they will be chased away and get nothing. The same applies to mares in foal, which require special attention.

Actually, provided you feed enough and well, almost any horse or pony can weather the winter out. But *fed it must be*, not just on hay alone.

The ice on water-troughs, etc., should be broken in frosty weather and a plentiful supply of water should *always* be available. Many owners seem to rely on puddles or small buckets, which quickly get knocked over. Water containers should be solid and fixed for this reason.

Rock salt is excellent, supplies many deficiencies and costs very little. Glucose licks are also beneficial and very popular.

STABLING AT RIDING HOLIDAY ESTABLISHMENTS

Stabling is a "must" in riding holiday centres of any repute. They need not be elaborate, although of course at the best centres they are all that is to be desired and a pleasure to see; but even the rougher ones can be adequate and can keep the horses comfortable. They can and should always be kept clean and tidy. Clean, tidy, well-kept stables and horses are more important than paint and polish, although both are ideal. Draughts should be avoided, and it is better to stand the horses and ponies with the windows and top doors wide open than to leave them in a draught. Fresh air is all-important; stuffy stables produce more ills than cold ones ever do. Ponies with their coats on or even clipped trace-high can be housed in open sheds in deep straw, which need not be mucked out daily but only "topped up". This makes for warmth, and as they are working by day, their feet come to no harm. But they must be fed individually or there will be kicking and biting, and feeding should be supervised or the bullies will get most of the food. With proper organization and supervision, peace can be maintained.

One can either buy an established going concern with goodwill and take the stock and equipment over at valuation, or buy lock, stock and barrel. In the latter case you cannot then reject any particular item but must take the rough with the smooth. A surveyor and a lawyer will also have to assess the amount of goodwill. Alternatively, you can buy or rent premises and build up your own goodwill. There are various ways of doing this.

1. Obtaining the essential grazing and erecting either permanent or portable buildings.

2. Obtaining the essential grazing and converting existing buildings.

3. Obtaining the land and stabling complete.

Location. Much thought should be given to the area, for unless it lies in good riding or trekking country and is also near a town or other means of supply, the income may fall far short of the outgoings and the establishment will quickly go bust—or (which, alas, is frequently the case), the animals you use will go short of food and shoes.

Essential Buildings

Looseboxes can of course be purchased at any of the well known firms but a good local joiner can make a suitable loosebox but it must be on a cement floor and have a drain running away from the yard. Every good establishment has a "dung heap" which if properly built and maintained is saleable, especially to mushroom growers.

You will also, of course, require a food store with tins to protect the food from rats and mice, and a tack room. This must be heated in winter or the leather will get mildew. A stove or safety electric fire is therefore essential.

Well run establishments have an office and the tack room should have brackets on which to hang each saddle and bridle with the name of the pony it fits—or should fit. Mangers save money as buckets or tins get knocked over and then food is wasted. Hay nets are better than racks but should be hung high and the rope attached to the bottom to prevent the animal getting its feet through the mesh.

Hot water must be available for tack cleaning.

There should be saddle- and bridle-racks, however crudely built, with the name of the animal above or below each, to ensure that each gets his own properly fitted equipment.

A saddle-horse is essential, as are bridle-cleaning hooks and other brackets on which to hang halters, etc.

If an electrically heated saddle-horse can be afforded it is a wonderful asset, but an ordinary one can be made by a local carpenter. Many of these articles can be obtained at sales. Keep all tack and equipment securely locked up, and have it insured.

Food Store. This too will have to be collected in rat-proof tins—dustbins will do—or most of the food will go to the rats or be so rat-run that no animals will eat it. Never leave food lying in the open. If it is possible, buy in bulk; this is always more economical. Above all, do not buy inferior food. Some means of obtaining hot water and of boiling food, such as linseed for mashes, is also an essential in well-run stables.

Office. An office, however small, is very necessary and adds prestige to an establishment when nicely and warmly furnished. It is essential for keeping accounts, records, answering the telephone and for interviewing clients. It also helps to keep clients out of the tack room at busy periods!

STABLING AT TREKKING CENTRES

Establishments catering only for trekking do not require elaborate stabling, but it is of great value in organizing a centre, especially a large one, if there are stalls in which to tie up the ponies, for feeding, saddling, grooming, etc.

If these stalls can be inside some large barn or old-fashioned stable this is ideal, as then all concerned are under cover from wind, rain and sun. Stalls can be fitted with single rails at little expense and the benefit of saddling and feeding under cover is obvious to anyone who has tried doing this in a high wind or a downpour of rain. To go out riding on a soaking wet pony is not pleasant. The ponies will be wet enough when first coming in of a morning from the fields, without standing out in the rain while they feed and the trekkers have their breakfast. At least under cover they dry off a little and may be saddled up without the saddle also getting wet.

If no shed or stable is available then the next best thing is a long railing, to which ponies can be tied, with an adequate space in between and, if possible, a tin roof overhead. The stalls are to be recommended, not only because of the shelter that is afforded, but to eliminate the risk of injury by kicking, etc. (Fig. 54).

Fig. 54. Ponies in stalls under cover

Tack Room. Where tack is stored for the winter, all leather should be treated with white Vaseline, Koa-chalin, or Flexalan or it will attract mildew. It is too much to hope that any heating will be available, though this is the ideal way to prevent mildew, which is incurable. But it should definitely be kept in a dry atmosphere. Once having contracted mildew, leather will always have it.

During this period all saddles should be restuffed and the linings mended, and all broken straps and buckles repaired. Girths should be washed and, if leather, put away carefully; bits and stirrup irons cleaned and polished. Hot water is therefore an asset.

Farrier

Every centre should be within easy reach of a good farrier. Any would-be operator would be well advised to make sure of this in the first place. No foot—no horse is the axiom he should remember. But to obtain one is increasingly difficult.

Every horse or pony should be shod every four to six weeks, according to the work he is doing and whether or not it is on soft ground or along roads. Even if the shoes are not worn out they should be removed, the hooves pared and the shoes refitted. Hot shoeing (that is where the farrier has a fire in which to heat the iron of the shoes) is of course best, but nowadays cold shoeing has to do. The danger here is that the farrier may pare the hoof to fit the shoe instead of making the shoe fit the hoof. Over-pared hooves are distressed hooves.

To leave a horse or pony with its hooves too long strains the back tendons and muscles of its legs (see Fig. 48). To have the clenches (nails) of the shoe protruding means they will bruise the leg on the opposite side or even cause deep wounds (see Fig. 48). Clenches can be knocked down without the aid of the farrier. Loose shoes should be seen to and no animal worked without shoes or even without one shoe. The weight of a shoe depends on the type of horse or pony and the work it is doing. To economize, some operators use very heavy shoes, which does not matter on trekking animals, but it is not good for riding holidays on light-limbed animals.

Animals that for any reason "brush", that is knock the leg with the opposite hoof or shoe must be specially shod with feathered-edge shoes, which then do not injure the opposite leg even if he is liable to do so (see Fig. 49). Weak, half-starved animals brush more readily than fit ones for obvious reasons. Others do what is called "forge", that is knock the front shoe with the tip of the back (Fig. 55); in this case the hind shoe would be set well back on the hoof to prevent this. Again, forging is a sign of weakness or "unbalance".

A good farrier can spare an operator many pounds. Nothing looks and is worse than to see animals from trekking or riding holiday centres with their feet long, their shoes worn or falling off and their legs and fetlocks bruised and bleeding through the shoes or nails knocking against them (see Fig. 48).

Mordax road studs are used in some instances to prevent slipping, especially if there is much road work or slippery

Fig. 55. Over-reach at trot

hillsides. Calkins (heels) should be made on both hind shoes of trekking ponies, again to prevent slipping.

Saddler

A "tame" saddler is also a great help. The most prevalent evil in riding establishments all over the country—sore backs—is due to the saddles not being re-stuffed or re-lined promptly, or to linings becoming worn (Fig. 38). It pays in the long run to repair them at once. Straps are forever getting broken and saddles damaged. To be able to have these repaired quickly is a great blessing. It is not right that trekkers or other riders should find themselves with reins that are broken or which come apart because the buckles are broken or lost.

MEDICINE CUPBOARD

Every stables, be it a trekking or riding holiday or riding school, should most certainly have an adequately supplied medicine cupboard containing such first-aid equipment as:

Gamgee—for wounds, to place under bandages when riding out on a horse with filled tendons or any other defects.

Lint.

Woollen bandages.

Cotton and crêpe bandages.

Bowl for water—for bathing wounds, etc.

Animal lintex or kaolin for poulticing.

Common salt as disinfectant and for hardening backs.

Lead lotion for sprains, etc.

Colic drinks (if a veterinary surgeon is not available quickly to give injections).

Derris powder for warbles.

Eucalyptus oil for streaming colds.

An electuary for coughs.

A thermometer.

A length of hose-pipe—for applying running water from the tap to strains and sprains.

Sulphanilamide powder—for wounds and galls.

Ointments for cracked heels and girth galls (but prevention is easier than cure!)

A twitch (experienced persons only).

Fuller's earth and vinegar—for bursal enlargements such as windgalls or capped hocks or thoroughpins.

Glucose—in case of illness.

Epsom or Glauber salts are tasteless and therefore acceptable.

Radiol—(M.R. muscle) from Boots or direct from Radiol Chemicals Ltd., 76 Upper Richmond Road, London, S.W.15.

Trainer's Wash. This can be made up as follows and applied to all sprains, strains, sore shins, etc. 2 oz., i.e. one wineglassful Radiol (M.R. muscle); 2 oz. (one wineglassful) vinegar; Radiol leg wash powder, 1 packet. Add 20 oz. water and shake well. (1 bottle of Radiol will make a gallon of wash.)
For conjunctivitis of the eyes caused by flies when animals are out at grass apply any antibiotic eye ointment. Neoprotosyl ointment is excellent if obtainable.
Boracic powder.
Pair of scissors.
Linseed oil: for use as a mild purgative, the dose is a pint to one and a half pints according to size of pony or horse; also for feeding to give a gloss to coats and put on fat.
Bicknall's Gall Cure.
Dettol.
Jeyes Fluid for disinfecting stables.
Friar's Balsam for coughs and also for disinfecting mangers in epidemics.
Benzyl Benzoate for sweet itch, obtainable from chemists.

QUALIFICATIONS OF PRINCIPAL OR OPERATOR, INSTRUCTORS AND STAFF

Trekking Centres

Every centre should have a really experienced, sensible and responsible person in charge and, if it is a large centre, an equally responsible staff under him or her. The instructor or guide in charge should preferably be a good mixer. Whoever it is, he or she will require infinite patience and tolerance to handle so many human beings and animals, all with varying experience and temperaments. Some riders may be nervous, others over-confident. Some will want to go slow, others will want to move faster, even to gallop, whereas trekking is intended to be undertaken at the walk or jog-trot.

The nervous rider will have to be looked after and encouraged.

Riding Holiday Establishments

It is very much better when the principal of a riding holiday establishment is fully qualified or has had long experience. If he or she has not this advantage and knowledge, someone who has should be employed. All teaching staff should have some qualification, either several years' experience in a good stable under good instructors or they should hold a Certificate from the British Horse Society. This is essential, not only for the safety of the clients but in order that the instruction, however elementary, should be on sound lines. As things are, people with no knowledge whatsoever themselves are giving instruction.

Practical experience is much more valuable than letters after one's name. Too many young girls go into stables without knowledge of any kind, which is all right as long as they are prepared to serve an apprenticeship, as in every other trade, but alas, many of them are only out for a "jolly". However, on the whole, girls are proving better than men because, if they are good, they take infinite trouble and really care about the animals in their charge.

Without practical experience no operator or instructor can know the sort of things that can happen. Experience also conveys confidence, which is the crux in sensible handling of both humans and animals. "Prevention is better than cure" should be the slogan over the door of every stable.

It is essential that trekking operators and their staff should know all about the ponies they are using, otherwise how can they suit the rider to the pony, which is another essential? In some establishments the operator hires the ponies either for the season, by the week, or as he requires them. They are brought to the trekking centre on the Monday morning and returned home for the week-end. Varying distances are therefore added to the mileage already done on "trek", which varies between five and twenty-five miles a day. It will be appreciated, therefore, that trekking ponies work hard and have long hours out of stable or field, which is known to be exacting. Moreover those which receive no extra rations have to find their own food at night, which leaves little time for them to lie down and rest, so that they get "leg weary". They are supplied complete with whatever saddle or bridle their owners put on them, which are often sadly lacking and rarely cleaned, so that the stuffing of the saddle both sinks and gets dirty, and the leather becomes hard and uncomfortable. Whereas operators who own their own ponies and equipment are often justly proud of them, less interest is naturally taken in hirelings. At the same time it is obviously difficult for operators with very large numbers to cater for to keep enough ponies of their own to meet a fluctuating demand, but as they pay well for a hireling, they can surely insist that the animal is fed, and the equipment good and properly maintained.

The type of animals which are the most economical and suitable for use in either trekking or riding holiday establishments have already been described in previous chapters.

CHAPTER X

Handling Horses and Ponies

SOME people are born with horse sense, some acquire it. Some think they know everything and they are invariably the most ignorant. Years of tradition have established certain unwritten laws. Here are some of them:

Speak often and quietly. Never approach a pony without first making your presence known to it. Speak before you move, not after.

Handle firmly, quietly and never roughly; but make sure the pony knows who is boss. Do not move suddenly or quickly. Never grasp a limb or even touch a pony's leg without first speaking· and putting your hand on neck or quarter. Work down the foreleg or towards the tail and down the hind-leg with stroking movements. Only a novice or a fool goes straight to a leg without first laying his hand on shoulder, neck or quarter and *speaking*. "Whoa, boy" or "Whoa, lass" or "There's a beauty" may sound silly but they are quite adequate. Single words are more efficacious than a sentence.

Never shout or brandish implements or stocks.

Never hit a pony about the head.

Approach a pony at its shoulder, not its quarter. Stroke the neck where its mother licked it when a foal, speaking all the time. If the pony moves ears backwards and forwards alternately and looks back, watch your step and keep well into his flank. Don't ask for trouble by getting behind him or he may lash out.

Ponies, like all animals, are creatures of habit. Regularity gives them a sense of security, so be regular. Feed at the same time every day. Regularity when dealing with all horses and ponies saves endless time and trouble and aids digestion.

Ponies love companionship, and all are gregarious. Much time and difficulty can be saved by remembering this. For instance, ponies are much quieter in a riding school—following-the-leader—than out on their own. But take them away from companions and there will probably be trouble. Novices should watch for this. The herd instinct plays an important part, especially with native breeds. It accounts for much, such as pawing the ground when feeding, turning the quarters when food is about, laying back the ears, kicking; for centuries it has been a question of survival of the fittest!

Fig. 56. Kicking, turning quarters and biting when fed outside in herds and young ponies get nothing

To tie up a pony for the first time, use unbreakable tackle at all costs and tie to a ring or post *that will not break.* If the youngster breaks away, he will probably be difficult to tie up for the rest of his life. Tie up short, as then he is less liable to get a leg over and otherwise hurt himself. Tie a quick release knot (see Fig. 5) in case of an emergency. Stand clear and let him fight it out, again giving plenty of bedding or soft falling under him. Use common sense in choosing a place to do this essential training. *Stay with him.*

To Lead a Pony

Most ponies lead best from the near (left) side, through habit. It is a good thing to try and teach them to lead from either hand.

Pick up rope or rein in right hand (back part of hand uppermost) to lead on the left. Grasp rope a short distance from the headstall or hemp halter with right hand and take up slack with the left hand. (Reverse instructions when leading from the right (off) side.) *Do not look back.* Horses and ponies dislike being stared in the face. Speak to the animal and move forward. If it refuses to move keep well in behind its shoulder and again invite it to move on, saying, "Walk on". If there is no response and the animal still hangs back, take a long, thin switch (a twig from a tree on the hedge will do, but it must be long), carry it in the left hand and use it on the animal's side behind your own back, where he cannot see it, at the same time inviting him to "walk on", then raising the right hand holding the rope or rein and again commanding him to "walk on". This he will probably do now. Always tie a knot under his chin when using a hemp halter.

When turning, first check slightly with rein and then turn *away* from yourself, not towards.

Use the same methods when inviting him to trot, but say "T-R-O-T ON".

Animals that are Hard to Catch

In the case of a confirmed sinner it is a good idea to take time to go out into the field and give the pony a feed and to stand quietly beside him while he eats it, making no attempt whatsoever to catch him. This should be repeated until his confidence is restored and he no longer associates a feed with being caught; thereafter approach him gradually and carefully in the manner described previously. It is quite hopeless once you start rounding up a pony with this tiresome habit, as this only makes him nervous and if he starts

galloping you have "had it". If, as sometimes happens, a
pony is impossible to catch, then I think a small enclosure
or shed must be erected in the field, into which he may be
persuaded to go if persistently fed therein. A headstall will
have to be left on always—although this is not desirable as
they can easily catch their legs in it when rolling or scratch-
ing, or even get caught up in a fence. A small end of rope
should be attached and left hanging down under the pony's
chin, which will make it slightly easier to get hold of him.

The advisability of teaching a pony or horse from the
start is stressed because of the time and trouble spent upon
those which contract this irritating habit—simply because at
some time or another, someone has gone the wrong way
about it.

Clipping

Never clip an animal which is out at grass unless you are
prepared to supply it with a New Zealand rug—and even
so it should only be clipped trace high. Never clip out either
a horse or a pony's legs or you will rue the day as it will
almost inevitably get cracked heels. Trace clipping prevents sweating and chill.

See that the clipper blades are sharp and so do not pull
the hair. This is the main cause of animals being difficult to
clip or "funny about their heads". Again take things quietly,
don't make the animal suspicious, keep the clipper head
flat and take care not to dig the teeth into the skin. Let the
machine do the clipping. Do not force the teeth through the
hair. Thick winter coats full of grease require very sharp
blades as the fine "cat" hairs get between the blade and
cause them to clog. Clean with paraffin, keep the animal's
loin covered while you clip out neck, shoulders and head,
and vice versa. Pass a damp water brush over the coat when
clipped to remove scurf; give a good strapping with body
brush and curry comb and rug up well.

Remember if using electricity that a horse or pony can
be killed if there is a "short" in the wiring. Should the
current be strong enough it need only touch the hair of his
tail as horses and ponies are very susceptible to electricity.

Aids

These are the signals by means of which a rider conveys to his mount what his intentions are and what he wishes it to do. The animal must be taught to obey them.

The means of producing these signals are of two kinds—natural aids, namely the hands by means of the reins, legs, body and voice; and artificial aids, namely whips, spurs, martingale, etc.

Natural Aids

1. Regulate the impulsion created by the application of the legs.

2. Control the forehand and guide, check and control the pace of the pony.

The Legs stimulate impulsion and create energy; guide and control the hindquarters.

The Body alters the distribution of weight by moving either forwards, backwards or sideways. The weight should, however, always be *slightly* inclined towards whichever way the pony and its rider are going. Rolling about in the saddle causes sores.

The Voice assists in controlling, encouraging, soothing and checking the pony. Conversely it can frighten it and greatly upset it.

All aids should work together for good.

Artificial Aids are whips and spurs, which should not be carried by novices who do not know their correct use.

Elements of Jumping

Nearly all ponies are natural jumpers, much "freer" than horses and, if properly ridden and shod and not sickened of it, enjoy jumping.

The reasons for ponies refusing to jump are:

1. Inexperience or being hustled over too large obstacles to start off with. Therefore place a log or pole on the ground and start walking over this. Raise slightly every day. But three foot six inches is quite high enough for any "school"

fence, even for experienced ponies. Otherwise they start refusing.

2. Over-facing a pony—that is asking him or forcing him to jump more and higher than he is capable of doing, or is strong or fit enough to undertake. It requires muscles to jump and grass-fed or "poor" ponies have none. It also requires *balance*. A pony should jump off his hocks and must be trained to do so or he will never be much good.

3. Getting "left behind" and so *jabbing in the mouth when*

Fig. 57. A happy, contented animal jumping

he does jump. Nothing stops a horse or pony quicker or sickens and disappoints him more—nor does he easily forget.

4. Don't sicken him. The best show jumpers are hardly jumped at all at home, and then only over small fences—the best training of all for a novice is to take him hunting and, when out riding, jump him over natural small obstacles like ditches, tree trunks or small rails, so that he comes to

enjoy it. Going over and over the same fences sickens intelligent animals, and ponies are notably intelligent.

5. Beating a horse or pony over fences when weak or young or green is not a pretty sight and is quite useless. You have to know when, how, and where to hit a horse before you do this sort of thing, and to do it on an animal that is not fit to do what you are asking it to do, is not only bad horsemanship, but cruel.

6. Children should not be allowed to jump perpetually and to ride about at shows, gymkhanas and rallies all day

Fig. 58. Unhappy, fighting the bit, whisking tail

long instead of getting off and resting the pony at every possible opportunity. Often the parents are to blame and are the worst offenders.

Neckstraps for Jumping. Novices and children should always be given a neckstrap to hang on by when learning to jump or even when learning to ride. Also, only snaffles should be used. Hold on to the neckstrap and not the animal's mouth or he will almost certainly refuse and/or throw his head up. So would you in his place. Wise trekking operators also provide this sensible aid when climbing up and down mountains, or use the halter rope.

Refusing. If he refuses, lower the jump to a height that he will accept, and begin all over again, raising it slightly each day until he regains his confidence. Do take time and don't go on and on.

Take him quietly, present him at the obstacle firmly and calmly without brandishing sticks. Throw your own heart over. If he knows—and he will—that you are certain you are both going to get over it, he will. Remember all the best riders are *quiet* riders. They consider their animals before themselves and would rather forgo prizes than over-do their ponies or horses.

The horses and ponies that look well, go quietly and freely and happily and jump willingly because they, too, enjoy it, are the lucky ones. They belong to people who realize the importance—not just of good horsemanship, but of good horse or pony*mastership*, i.e. the care and understanding of horses and ponies—not just the riding of them.

The unlucky horses and ponies are those which have a sad look in their eyes or else a scared one—they go with their heads down or else right up in the air, they fight for their .heads and cross their jaws against the pressure of the bit which is hurting them; their tails swish with irritation, they lay their ears back instead of pricking them eagerly, they stick their toes in or kick against the stick they are only too accustomed to, or against the spurs whose marks you can see long after the pricks have actually healed. Every picture tells a story!

You Should Notice

You will know that your horse or pony is well and healthy if his head is alert, ears pricked and warm, eyes open and bright, nostrils round and normal (not squared and distended); his head will turn towards you as you approach. Forelegs should stand firmly on the ground, but one hind leg may be resting. Legs should be cool, coat lying down and glossy, stomach normal, breathing regular—the flanks rising and falling about sixteen times a minute (double flank movement is a sign of broken wind); bowels should move about ten times in twenty-four hours; droppings soft enough to break when they fall unless animal is out on lush or wet grass when they will be loose and a greenish colour. Neck should be firm and rounded—even crested—and glossy; back and loin muscled up with no ribs or hip bones showing; quarters rounded with no groove (called "poverty line") running down them from tail to hock.

On the other hand, you can be pretty sure an animal is tired and "leg weary" if he stands with his head down, sometimes between his knees, resting alternate legs, his eyes are dull and his ears back. If he is definitely not well his ears may be cold, his coat standing up and "starey", his breathing fast and irregular, his pulse quick and his temperature above normal. His droppings may be hard or conversely loose through no just cause, or there may be a stoppage. He may have a discharge from his nostrils—a sign of a cold or cough—pain in his stomach (colic), or he may stand pointing a front toe which can be a sign of lameness, or else with his legs stretched out in an endeavour to take the weight off his heels—a sure sign of foot trouble. If he has an attack of colic he will turn round and look anxiously at his flanks, kick up at his stomach which may be hard and distended; get down and roll, rise and get down again, according to the spasms. If this happens out riding you should get off him and remove the saddle. In any case report to the person in charge who should either, as quickly as possible, administer a colic drench or get a veterinary surgeon to inject the animal. He should then be walked quietly round to help the medicine work. Should the attack last more than six hours there is cause for alarm, but usually whatever causes the trouble or the stoppage is passed through the bowels before this, when the animal should be given only warm bran mashes or good sweet meadow hay for twenty-four hours, and not worked for at least forty-eight hours. Avoid mouldy hay, which is often the cause.

If your mount when out riding appears to wish to stop, he may want to "stale" (pass water) and should be allowed to do so, when the rider should stand up in his stirrups and lean forward to take the weight off the kidneys.

If a horse or pony suddenly refuses to eat, suspect either sore throat or laryngitis, tooth trouble, a temperature, or "off colour" from some cause.

Never refuse to let any animal drink when he wishes to do so, whether in the stable or field or out riding, unless you are proceeding at really fast paces, when water should be given on returning home. It is cruel and uneconomical to keep horses and ponies short of water, which should be available to them at all times.

If your mount suddenly starts bucking, there may be something hurting or nipping him under the saddle or girths, so do not blame him but remove the cause. If you find a lump on his back it may be caused by an ill-fitting saddle which, if you continue to ride him, may develop into a sore or even an ulcer. It may, however, only be that a warble fly has laid an egg there the previous summer when the lump will be a maggot. Report this if not already being treated, and do not ride the animal if the back is tender. He will shiver and sink down when you touch his back if it is. Look to your pony's shoes to see if they are secure and the clenches (nails) not sticking out, when they are liable to bruise and wound the opposite leg.

If your horse or pony is very lively and shies at imaginary or real objects, and humps his back, then he is what is called "fresh". After he has worked for a while he will probably settle down. Don't, however, hesitate to tell the instructor if you are at all nervous or to ask for his help and advice at all times. There is nothing to be ashamed of in seeking advice and help. The best riders have all done it at one time or another.

Summing Up

All this may have sounded rather alarming and difficult, but tackled with determination and common sense, it will add to your interest and therefore enjoyment to know just a little about the horses and ponies which share this wonderful and unique adventure.

Once having come to terms with your pony, be he a

Highlander, a Fell or a Dales or just an endearing "mongrel", having lost your nervousness and even developed an affection for rotund Maisie, cunning old Tubby, or the winsome and sturdy Taffy from Wales, you will find an extraordinary exhilaration in plodding up and slithering down mountains in a Scottish mist, or wading through reddening bracken or rushing streams, with Mac dexterously snatching at the fronds as you go or stopping to blow bubbles. The silver birches with the sun shining on their mottled trunks resemble some wonderful stage set, and, lying relaxed on the spring-time heather upon upland grass—soft as a Vi-spring mattress—you will find yourself dreaming of nothing in particular instead of worrying about mundane matters:

> "Each day it's the same, I can scribble my name,
>   In the dust on the sitting-room table,
>   I don't dare to think of the scullery sink,
>   Or what I shall do without Mabel!"

All these irritations will pass from you. You will find yourself transported from the kitchen to the mountain top. Sitting on a perfect summer's day on the heathered slopes above a Highland loch, or beside the waters which reflect the hills in the Lake District, listening to the murmur of voices and the cropping of the ponies as they graze beside you, you forget that you ever had a vacuum cleaner or an electric iron, a job that gets you down, or that, only a week ago, you felt tired and ill and bored. Now you are "back to nature" you get a true perspective.

By now, too, you will have forgiven Mac for standing on your toe while eating his breakfast, or for moving every time you attempted to mount. You and your companions have had a good laugh recalling how, when he put his head down to grab a luscious bite of grass you very nearly tobogganed down his neck!

Trailing leisurely homeward in the gloaming through pine-scented forests, you will anticipate the gorgeous hot bath to come, that orange you will suck in it, and the cup of tea and ham and eggs to follow. Sitting in the lounge of some gay and friendly inn with the new friends you have made, you talk over the day's adventures, as huntsmen do a day's sport. The mountains get bigger, the rivers deeper, the bogs more dangerous as the night proceeds. And if you have fallen off during the day—and got on again—you will find yourself the hero of the party!

And so to the end of a perfect holiday—

> "Time passed and with it took Romance,
> But left me with the happy chance,
> To see what Fortune held in store,
> In pastures I'd ne'er trod before."

Good luck to you with your trekking and your riding holidays, and with your horses and ponies. Treat them kindly but firmly. Don't be daft with them or they will take advantage of you as children do. They can be a great source of pleasure and satisfaction and there is no better way of teaching young people initiative, courage, method, sensibility, and consideration for others.

We have the best ponies and horses in the world. Let us also earn and deserve the reputation of being the best horse- and ponymasters.

Index